SKETCHES OF INDIA

SKETCHES OF INDIA

WITH NOTES ON THE SEASONS, SCENERY AND SOCIETY OF BOMBAY, ELEPHANTA, AND SALSETTE

HENRY MOSES

GYAN

Published by

Gyan Publishing House
5, Ansari Road
Daryaganj, New Delhi-110002
Phone: 011-47034999, 9811692060
E-mail: books@gyanbooks.com

Distribution Network
gyanbooks.com
India, USA, Canada, UK, Australia

ISBN: 978-93-7447-600-0 (PB)

First Published, 1750

2nd Impression 2026

Printed at: Gyan Press, Delhi.

SKETCHES OF INDIA
Author: HENRY MOSES

SKETCHES OF INDIA.

Drawn by W. Daniell, R.A. Engraved by J. Stephenson.

Bombay

SKETCHES OF INDIA:

WITH NOTES ON THE

SEASONS, SCENERY, AND SOCIETY

OF

BOMBAY, ELEPHANTA, AND SALSETTE.

BY

HENRY MOSES, M.D.

I pity the man who can travel from Dan to Beersheba, and cry, 'tis all barren—and so it is; and so is all the world to him who will not cultivate the fruits it offers.—STERNE.

LONDON:
PUBLISHED BY SIMPKIN, MARSHALL & Co.
STATIONERS' HALL COURT.

MDCCL.

OPINIONS OF THE PRESS.

"Full of amusing anecdote."

[Here follow extracts from the "Island of Elephanta."]

Plymouth and Devonport Herald, May 6, 1848.

"A most graphic description of the setting in of the south-west monsoons."

Banner of Ulster, Dec. 1847.

"A very interesting paper on the hot season; its continuation in August gives many details of the manners and customs of India."

[Here follow extracts.]

Plymouth Herald, Aug. 5, 1848.

"Dr. H. Moses' Sketches of Eastern scenery and manners are graphic and interesting."

Maidstone Journal, Aug. 28, 1848.

DEDICATION.

TO

MRS. MILNER.

DEAR MADAM,

In availing myself of your permission to dedicate to you the following "Sketches of India," I need scarcely say how highly I appreciate the kindness of that permission; or how deeply I am gratified, by the favourable opinion which you have manifested of my work, by giving to the substance of the following pages insertion in "The Englishwoman's Magazine." It is impossible not to feel the value of approbation when it proceeds from such a quarter.

I am, madam,

With every feeling of respect and esteem,

Your obedient servant,

HENRY MOSES.

PREFACE.

The following "Sketches of India," were originally introduced to the notice of the public through the medium of "The Englishwoman's Magazine." They are now published in a separate form, in consequence of the solicitation of friends, to whose judgment, warped though it may be by feelings of personal regard, I cannot but defer.

It may be proper to observe, as affording some guarantee for the correctness of these sketches of the seasons, scenery, and society of Bombay, that they have been compiled from copious notes, made during a sojourn in that island. I have myself seen all that I have here attempted to describe; and, with an especial view to the benefit of those youthful readers to whom authentic accounts of foreign lands are, generally peculiarly attractive, I have endeavoured while treating of "the clime of the East," to lead their minds to the contemplation of Him, whose goodness and greatness are reflected in the grace and beauty, with which, in that fair clime, external nature is so profusely adorned.

The moral and religious condition of India, must, of course, constitute a topic too important to be omitted, even in the slightest or most desultory account of that country. India is now ripe for the sickle; but, alas! the mighty harvest of ignorance and superstition has yet to be gathered in.

I would add, in conclusion, that if I be thought to have lingered too long upon "the voyage out;" or to have dwelt with needless minuteness on matters which have often been described by travellers bound for the East; my apology must be, that having been myself deeply impressed by the ever-changing scenes which the ocean, during a long voyage, never fails to present to the observant spectator, I have been anxious to communicate some idea of those scenes to my readers, and more especially to the younger portion of them; being persuaded, that the impressions produced upon the mind by the wonders of "the Great Deep," are no less salutary than they are vivid and abiding.

HENRY MOSES.

Appleby, Westmoreland, April, 1850.

CONTENTS.

CHAPTER I.

CHAPTER II.

CHAPTER III.

CHAPTER IV.

CHAPTER V.

CHAPTER VI.

CHAPTER X.

CHAPTER XI.

RECOLLECTIONS OF INDIA.

CHAPTER I.

"Roll on, thou deep and dark blue ocean—roll!
Ten thousand fleets sweep over thee in vain;
Man marks the earth with ruin—his control
Stops with the shore; upon the watery plain
The wrecks are all thy deed, nor doth remain
A shadow of man's ravage, save his own,
When, for a moment, like a drop of rain,
He sinks into thy depths with bubbling groan—
Without a grave, unknelled, uncoffined, and unknown."

BYRON.

Introduction Glance at Porto Santo. Procellaria pelagica. Their food and habits. Halothuria Physalis. Exocetus Volitans. Their visits to the English coast. Vast fields of Sea-weed. A man overboard. Madagascar at Sun-set. Search after the lost boy. Sorrow of the crew. Have the sharks eaten him? Sunday on the ocean. Our sea service. The Sesostris steam-Frigate. Her deck passengers. Bombay harbour. Land Sharks and servants. First impressions of India. Vasco del Gama. Moguls. Portuguese and Charles the Second. Situation of Bombay. Strange people. Goa. What have we done for India? Reflections, &c., &c., &c.

A VOYAGE to India has often been described; and there is, in truth, little variety in the every-day scenes on board a large vessel. The passengers you meet with are pretty much of the same stamp, and have been depicted, times out of number, by the thousand and one voyagers to the East, who have given us amusing portraits of the old officer returning to join his regiment after a leave of absence; and of the young cadet, fresh from the military college of Addiscombe, with his head full of the Wellington despatches, and of Bengal tigers. According to the good old custom, I kept an accurate diary, and was as punctual in noting down every little event, as our first mate was in recording in his log-book the progress of the ship, or the state of the weather every twenty-four hours. In turning over the leaves of this diary, I find but little worth extracting. It is but a record of sunshine and storms, and of many sad reflections upon taking leave of all that was near or dear to me on earth. The journal of my first week on board ship presents a dreary catalogue of troubles, occasioned by the loss of masts and sails in a gale of wind coming down channel—by the sea pouring in through the seams of the deck, and deluging my bed and cabin—and by other discomforts peculiar to new ships that have been fitted out in a hurry, and with but little regard to the comfort or convenience of those destined to live so many months on board of them. But these treats were of short duration; and a few fine days set us all to rights again. The carpenter, a clever and active man, was not long in completing the new spars to supply the place of those carried away, and our cabins were effectually secured against any further intrusions of the sea. Our crew consisted of a mixture of English, Irish, and Scotch sailors; and we had not been long on board, before the captain discovered that there were two or three bad characters amongst them. One morning, as we were sitting at breakfast, he was summoned on deck, and informed by these men who had been selected as spokesmen by the rest, that it was their determination to work only in their watch; that he was quite at liberty to confine them below deck if he thought proper, but work at any other time they would not. Having delivered this piece of information, the mutineers returned to the forecastle, and the captain very coolly sate down again and finished his cup of coffee with us in the cabin. So soon as the cloth was drawn, the mate was ordered to get the irons out—to load with ball three pistols—and to see that cutlasses were placed conveniently in every state-room in case they should be wanted in a hurry. Having finished these warlike preparations, we waited the issue of the afternoon's watch, to see if the crew would turn out as usual to their duty. Two bells were at last struck, and much to our surprise every hand appeared on deck. The malcontents saw that they had a determined character to deal with in the person of Captain W., and had thought it better to attend to his orders at once. As a punishment, he gave them all an extra hour's work; and the two ringleaders were set to holy-stone the decks until they begged his pardon. One condescended to do this the following morning, but the other rebel laboured at this hard and distasteful work for eight days, before his spirit was sufficiently broken to induce him to ask forgiveness for past offences. Thus was harmony and good order once more restored on board our vessel, and I am happy to say it was not interrupted again during the voyage. As we had a good library on board my time was profitably passed in reading and in noting down every event that had the slightest novelty to recommend it to notice; for the sea has a thousand charms to those who travel for instruction, or with a laudable desire to increase their acquaintance with the world which they inhabit; and though a long voyage may eventually tire the most sanguine inquirer in the pursuit of knowledge, yet a large and marvellous page of nature is open to him whose business is in the great waters. Of such a man it may truly be said, that he shall "see the wonders of the Lord." The change of temperature which begins to be very perceptible as you draw near the lovely group of the Madeiras when you first put on the cool white dress and enjoy your walk upon the high poop, is a pleasing relief after the fogs, rains, and chilly nights, which have depressed your spirits, and made you dissatisfied with everything. The young voyager is now delighted with the different colours of the sea. When viewed in hazy weather, a yellow tinge is spread over it; but, as he enters the torrid zone, a dark brown is the prevailing colour. But these hues are continually changing, for the bottom of the ocean has a wonderful influence over them; and the reflection of the sun, when the sky is clear and serene, decks the mighty expanse in the most refreshing green. When he reflects that this immense body of water which surrounds him occupies a space on the surface of our globe greater than that which is called dry land, and covers an extent of 148,000,000 of square miles, he is lost in the contemplation of so sublime a work. Again, there is his old welcome friend, the calm, pale moon—which always appears to the English eye unusually large when viewed through the clear tropical atmosphere—looking so bright and beautiful, that you scarcely know her again. Everything, in fact, that you see, as the ship steals through the waste of waters towards its destination, has a freshness and novelty about it which delights and enchants those who are interested in the wonderful works of God. To quote the words of the illustrious Humboldt, "one experiences an indescribable sensation when, as we approach the equator, and especially in passing from one hemisphere to the other, we see the stars, with which we have been familiar from infancy, gradually approach the horizon, and finally disappear. Nothing impresses more vividly on the mind of the traveller, the vast distance which separates him from his native country than the sight of a new firmament. The grouping of the large stars, the scattered nebulæ rivalling in lustre the milky-way, together with some spaces remarkable for their extreme darkness, give the southern heavens a peculiar aspect. The sight even strikes the imagination of those who, although ignorant of astronomy, find pleasure in contemplating the celestial vault, as one admires a fine landscape or a majestic site. Without being a botanist, the traveller knows the torrid zone by the mere sight of its vegetation; and, without the possession of astronomical knowledge, perceives that he is not in Europe, when he sees rising in the horizon the great constellation of the Ship, or the phosphorescent clouds of Magellan. In the equinoctial regions, the earth, the sky, and all their garniture, assume an exotic character."

It was a lovely morning that revealed to me the beauties of Porto Santo, the first land which we had seen since bidding adieu to dear happy old England. The pangs of separation had in a great measure passed away, and I now began to look more soberly upon my present lot—trusting alone to the goodness of Him who could cast it in pleasant places. I went on deck at 6 A. M., and ascertained from our second mate, who had charge of the watch, that we were only eight miles from the shore. I cannot conceive a more lovely picture than this singular island presented as the rising sun illumined the peaks of its lofty mountains, and dispelled the mists that still floated in fleecy clouds over its tranquil vallies. There are several small islands scattered about Porto Santo, and they all appear to be the work of some volcanic eruption. Porto Santo is, I believe, the smallest inhabited island of the Madeira group. It produces little corn, but its vallies feed numbers of oxen, and wild hogs are found on its hills. Its exports are few, and chiefly consist of wax, honey, and dragons' blood; while a small grape supplies a poor thin wine to its Portuguese cultivators. We saw Madeira, that grave of England's consumptive children, in the distance, but could form no idea of its extent or elevation. As the wind had died away, we were becalmed many hours under the lea of this land. The sky was cloudless, and the sea so clear and transparent, that the eye could penetrate many fathoms into the depths below. About 3 P. M. the thermometer fell rapidly, and all hands were ordered on deck, to prepare for a coming squall. Fortunately the wind was in our favour, and the sudden appearance of Mother-Cary's chickens, congregating under the stern of our vessel, confirmed the captain in his former belief that the fine morning was only a *foxy* one, and we might still expect a continuance of boisterous weather. A few words about the stormy petrel of these seas may prove acceptable to some of my younger readers. The procellaria pelagica is a pretty little bird, about six inches in length; with head, back, and tail, of a coal black tint, and with a broad transverse bar of white on the rump. The scapulars and secondary quills are tipped with white. It delights to skim the waves of the boundless Atlantic, and flies so near the surface as to appear as if running upon the water. These birds feed principally upon the small marine molusca, &c., that are cast upon the surface. I have observed them in the most awful storms, when it was scarcely possible for a man to stand upon deck from the fury of the gale.

> " Up and down! up and down!
> From the base of the wave to the billow's crown,
> And amidst the flashing and feathery foam,
> The Stormy Petrel finds a home :—
> A home, if such a place may be
> For her who lives on the wide, wide sea,
> On the craggy ice, in the frozen air,
> And only seeketh her rocky lair
> To warm her young, and teach them to spring
> At once o'er the waves on their stormy wing !"

The stormy petrels congregate under the sheltered sides of vessels, where they are in a great measure protected from the wind, and find plenty of food raised up by the action of the rudder, and upon the refuse thrown overboard from the cook's galley.—They have the power of ejecting from their stomachs an oily and fœtid matter. These birds are easily caught with a pin or fly-hook, baited with a piece of fat pork, trailed over the side or in the wake of the ship, from a thin line. Sailors have a superstitious veneration for these little wanderers of the deep, as they fancy their appearance prognosticates foul weather. But I have observed them on the finest days, and even when we were becalmed upon the line.—Ornithologists have described four varieties. One, the procellaria leechi, has a fine forked tail, and was first discovered by Mr. Bullock in the Island of Saint Kilda, whither many of the species resort in the breeding season. The nest of the procellaria pelagica is placed among loose stones, where a single egg of pure white is laid in the month of May. They have been found in many parts of the islands north of Scotland, and on the coast of the Isle of Man, but quit these stations in October or November, for warmer latitudes. Having passed the Deserters, another picturesque group of islands connected with Madeira, the next fresh object that engrossed my attention was the holothuria physalis, or little men-of-war, as they are commonly called by nautical people, from their resemblance to a vessel under canvas. We must have sailed through thousands of them in an hour.—They all had their little sails expanded, and were steering in the same direction as our ship. Their sail is a thin, semi-transparent membrane, extending diagonally from one side of the animal to the other.—When examined in a tub of water, on deck, it appeared to be almost white; but in certain lights, and in its native element, its edges are tinged by the most brilliant blue and crimson reflections. From the body are suspended numerous hair-like tentacula, or feelers, that are constantly engaged in entangling the food upon which the animal lives. When disturbed in the water, the sail is rapidly folded up, and the little man-of-war sinks out of sight. We caught many of them in a bucket; but I was charged not to handle them incautiously, as they would sting me, or paralyse the arm for some hours after. I was surprised to see these frail and delicate little creatures mounting securely over the lofty billows, though a brisk breeze was carrying us along at the rate of seven or eight knots an hour. I must not omit in my catalogue the beautiful flying-fish (*exocetus volitans*), so often described by travellers. Five days after our departure from Porto Santo, we got into their track, and saw shoals of them springing into the air, a height of ten or twelve feet. They would then flutter horizontally some distance, and then drop heavily into the ocean. The large pectoral fins act as wings to this animal; and as the swimming or air bladder is of unusual size for so small a fish, their extreme buoyancy in the atmosphere is easily accounted for. The flying-fish has many enemies. The dolphin, albacore, boneta, &c., are waging incessant war with them in the sea; and no sooner do they take to flight, than the prowling frigate-bird, or wide-awake, is ready to dash down among them, and drive them once more to seek shelter in their own native element. Some of our crew were very anxious to attract a few on board of our vessel; and during the night one or two of them got into the chains, and held a lantern out for that purpose; but after an hour's patient watching, the plan was given up, though said to be at times a very successful one. The following night, three or four fish flew across the ship, and three of them striking the sails, fell dead upon deck, and were served up the next morning for breakfast. The one I partook of was about ten inches long, and though nicely dressed, had little flavour or firmness to recommend it as an article of diet. We have a few instances on record of the flying-fish visiting our English seas. Pennant informs us that a fish of this genus was caught in June, 1765, at a small distance below Caermarthen, in the river Towy; and Jenning states that a second specimen was taken in July, 1823, in the Bristol Channel, ten miles from Bridgewater. In August, 1825, many were seen off Portland Island, by a vessel outward bound. The air in the swimming-bladder of the flying-fish has been supposed to be pure oxygen; but Baron Humboldt found it to consist of ninety-four parts of azote, two of carbonic acid, and only four of oxygen.

The close and dawn of day within the tropics present many magnificent sights to a spectator on shipboard. The brilliant constellations visible in more southern latitudes—the brief though fearful storm—the soul-depressing calms so often encountered on the line, and the strange and solitary birds that hover around your course, hundred of miles from any known land—all supply food to the imagination, and tend to elevate the mind to the Great Author and Governor of all things. It may be a little out of place here to speak of what we saw on the return voyage; but I cannot refrain from alluding to the vast fields of sea-weed that for two days so surrounded our vessel, as almost to impede its progress through the water.—This floating fucus is supposed to be detached by storms from the sub-marine rocks on which it is said to grow; but that which we fished up presented all the appearance of belonging to a healthy growing plant; nor could I detect any roots, &c., which might have induced me to suppose that it had been once attached to the rocky bottom of the ocean. Our captain said it was carried by the great current out of the Gulf of Mexico; but there is no foundation for this supposition. Many of the sailors appeared to be quite familiar with its appearance, eat large quantities of it, and said it was the tropic grape that grew in Neptune's vineyard, and cured all diseases. Two great banks of this singular, stringy-looking weed are said to occur in the Atlantic Ocean. One of them is often met with to the west of the meridian of Fayal, one of the Azores, but the site of the other has not been correctly ascertained. Burnet tells us, that it vegetates within forty degrees of latitude on each side the equator, and that vessels homeward bound from Monte Video or the Cape, always pass through one field of it. It was known to the Phœnicians as the Weedy Sea, and the Spaniards and Portuguese call it Mar de Zaragossa. It is related of Columbus, that the sailors who attended him on his first voyage of discovery to America, on passing through these fields of sea-weed, urged him to proceed no further on the voyage, but to return home again, as they superstitiously believed that this hindrance was designed by God to put a stop to his wild schemes.

It is astonishing what a trifle will create a bustle, and afford fresh subject for conversation at sea. A dead whale floating past, a ship in the distance, a passing shower, or even a shooting-star—all come in for their share of discussion and debate; for a ship's company, generally speaking, are garrulous, and fond of making the most of everything that may occur to break in upon the monotony of a long voyage. Calms are favourable seasons for conversation, which is often, as I have remarked, of a somewhat melancholy and dispiriting character. Few persons can form an idea of the dreadful gloom that is cast over a ship's crew when a death occurs on board; and more particularly so, when that death has been accidental! I had once the misfortune to be a participator in a scene of this sad description, and to be aroused from my bed by the fearful announcement— "A man overboard!" We were creeping quietly along the eastern coast of Madagascar, and had been amusing ourselves, the evening before, by viewing from the poop that large and mountainous island, through a powerful telescope. We had first sighted it at noon, and the varied scenery was continually changing, as, with a light breeze, we stole onwards. Not being very far from the coast, we could easily descry, even with the naked eye, fires blazing upon the shore, and objects moving around them. The mate, who appeared to be gifted with a remarkably long vision, and who saw through his glass things which no one else could see, declared that a human sacrifice was going forward at a particular spot named, and it was amusing to watch the anxiety of the apprentice boys to witness this extraordinary scene, and to obtain permission to look through the glass at the cannibals. I shall never forget the picturesque appearance of the mountains; bathed as their strange and ragged forms were in the rich hues of sunset. Some of these lofty hills tapered to a point; others bore an odd resemblance to towers or gigantic columns. As far as the eye could reach, mountains overtopped mountains, till the summits were undistinguishable in the purple haze of approaching night. I sat on the quarter-deck for some hours, watching this moving panorama; until at length darkness pitilessly shut out the lovely prospect. We had all been very merry that day, for we had caught the trade wind again; and the captain had welcomed the meeting with a bottle of noble champaign at dinner. The crew had an extra allowance of grog, and the boys had something very tempting for supper. Between two and three the following morning, I was disturbed by an unusual noise on deck, and by a great deal of running to and fro on the poop, over my little cabin. I sprang out of bed, and hastened on deck to inquire the cause; feeling, to say the truth, a little alarmed; for just about nightfall, there had passed us pretty close, a suspicious looking craft, which the captain took to be either a pirate or a slaver from the African coast. She burnt for a few minutes a white light at her bow, but never, as is customary with honest vessels, attempted to speak us. The second mate, whom I found in the greatest distress, told me that an apprentice—the poor boy's name was Morgan—had fallen overboard, from some part of the rigging near the cross-trees. He was seen to strike the rail in his descent. A small step-ladder was immediately thrown over to him, and the alarm being given, one of the boats was lowered down from the davits, four or five of the crew jumped into it half naked, and pulled off in the direction in which it was supposed the boy would be carried by the current. The night was not very dark. Some bright stars were visible; yet there was a good deal of thick haze floating over the sea. The ship of course was put about; and but a few minutes had elapsed before every hand had turned out, and every eye was strained to catch a glimpse of the boat, which had disappeared in the fog. It was an anxious moment to all on board. No one spoke above a whisper. Occasionally the splash of the oars was heard, and the deep voice of the man who steered, calling "Morgan! Morgan!" reached the ear; but poor Morgan was never more to obey his summons; he had received one from higher authority; the deep, deep sea, had closed over his body; and his spirit had departed to Him who gave it. Sorrow was depicted upon the countenances of all, when the brave boatmen came on board without him, and after securing the boat, crept off one by one in silence to their hammocks. They had picked up the ladder, but not the boy. I returned to my cabin, but not to sleep. My mind was too full of the image of our departed shipmate. He, an only child, was a poor sickly lad, and had been my first patient on board. I thought of his poor mother, till the picture was too painful to be dwelt upon; so I got up and returned to the deck, which I paced till daybreak, feeling revived by the cool night wind, that had rather increased during the last few hours. As the white spray dashed from the bows, I more than once fancied I heard poor Morgan's voice, calling from the angry waters below me. The old grey-headed boatswain was huddled up behind the large water-cask, in a great monkey jacket, for he had gone fast asleep after the trouble and exertion of the search for the lost boy. How easily, I thought, do some men take these awful warnings to be prepared for death! The mate joined me on deck; and we walked there together conversing on the uncertainty of life, till the shades of night were swept from off the bosom of the now beautiful ocean. The air was delicious, and Madagascar no longer visible to us. A few albatrosses, those mighty inhabitants of these regions, kept us company; and some stray Cape pigeons uttered their piercing little cry, as they followed in the wake of the vessel, and picked up the morsels of bread which the black cook seemed to take pleasure in throwing to them. The heavy dews of the past eventful night were still dripping from the sails and ropes; the dogs crept out from under the long boat, and shook their shaggy coats; the sleepers were awakened, and all was once more bustle and activity. Day had returned to the world, and man accordingly went "forth to his work and to his labour." The fine trade wind diverted our attention, and compelled us, as it were, to forget the lost boy who had been taken from amongst us. Troubles, it has been said, sit lightly on sailors; but we had on board a little cabin-boy, who had been a great friend of poor Morgan, and who bitterly felt his loss. In the course of the morning this poor lad came up to me on the quarter-deck, and, after looking at me very earnestly, asked, with much simplicity, whether I thought poor Tom was eaten by the sharks by this time. There was something so strange in the question, and in the child-like manner of putting it, that I felt, for an instant, at a loss how to reply. After a moment's silence, I told him, that, by the mercy of God, and through the merits of Jesus Christ our Saviour, poor Morgan was, I hoped, in a better world; and that, if so, it was of very little consequence to him whether he was eaten by the sharks at sea, or by the worms on shore; that our bibles told us, that at the last day, the sea would give up its dead, and that poor Morgan would not be forgotten. The little cabin-boy cried very bitterly; nor did anything that I could say, appear to comfort him. He was only twelve years of age, and an interesting and well-disposed boy. He could not read very well; but the black cook had taken some pains to teach him and poor Morgan to read the New Testament.

For several days a cloud was cast over the usual cheerfulness of the ship's crew. The fiddle in the forecastle was silent, and the hearty laugh was heard no more—sailors are proverbially superstitious, especially about death! I was told, that some of the crew fully expected to see the ghost of poor Morgan sitting on the bowsprit on the ninth night from his death. The following Sunday, it was pleasing to see that, out of respect to the departed youth, almost every man wore some article of mourning.

Speaking of Sunday, it is not a day often neglected, nor are its sacred hours allowed to pass by unheeded on ship-board; and though the beautiful prayers in our fine church service, intended for use at sea, are not always read aloud in the cabin of every vessel, yet I think, generally speaking, the Sabbath, in our English ships, is as well observed, and is kept as holy, as circumstances will admit. In this matter, everything of course depends upon the captain, who has many blessed opportunities of doing good to those entrusted to his care. I am now, it must be understood, speaking with reference to the Merchant Service; that great nursery for British seamen. The first Sabbath that I spent at sea is still fresh in my memory. The evening before exhibited quite a busy scene, and newly-washed clothes were fluttering from every rope, to dry. All the crew were engaged in setting matters in order on board; and on the following morning, all turned out in their best apparel. Everything connected with the usual daily work on board a large vessel was put out of sight, and the ends of all loose ropes were, what is called, "Flemish coiled." The decks, from the holy-stoning of the night before, were snowy-white; all unnecessary labour was avoided, and the men and boys were allowed as much spare time for reading as was consistent with the safe-working of the ship. It was a pleasing sight to see them seated at their ease, many reading their Bibles, or other books suitable to the day. Thoughtless as sailors too often are, the Bible is a book generally to be found in some corner of each man's chest; and it is not an unusual thing to see there also a bundle or two of religious tracts, put in, no doubt, by some good mother or sister, who had packed the box. On the day to which I allude, the captain said he would have prayers read in the cabin. All the boys were very properly ordered to attend, but the men were allowed to act in this matter as they thought proper; and the mate rang the bell at eleven o'clock. The morning was unusually calm and serene, and was singularly favourable to the performance of a duty of this description. I think all who could do so, attended the summons; and it gave me great pleasure to see so many of our most careless sailors fall down upon their knees as they entered the place set apart for prayer, and behave with all reverence during the whole service. There was something to me very impressive and beautiful in the appearance of this little group of persons, bound upon a long and dangerous voyage, and now voluntarily collected together in a frail vessel, and upon a treacherous sea, to offer up their prayers, and to pour forth their praises and thanksgivings before the throne of Him, whose paths are in the great waters, and whose footsteps are not known.

When the solemn introductory prayer was read, beginning with "O Eternal Lord God, who alone spreadest out the heavens, and rulest the raging of the sea, who hast compassed the waters with bounds, until day and night come to an end, be pleased to receive into thy Almighty and gracious protection, the persons of us thy servants," &c.; and when the reader proceeded to "thou didst send forth thy commandment, and the windy storm ceased and was turned into a calm," how little did any of us think, during that quiet and peaceful morning, when the elements were at rest, that in a few hours afterwards our vessel was to be nearly dismasted in a tremendous gale. Such, however, was the case. Within but a few hours, a storm burst upon us so suddenly, and with such awful fury, that before we could take in any canvass to save them, our main-topmast, main top-gallant mast and royal, were carried away. So little can they, who "have business in great waters," judge what an hour may bring forth.

But I have rambled from my purpose, and must return to it, or we shall never reach Bombay. When we were within a few days' sail of India, we were rudely summoned, by the commander of the Sesostris steamer, to heave-to, and bear tidings to the great men of Bombay, that she, the Sesostris steamer-frigate, had been out six days in a hurricane, but had weathered the gale, and was now going safely, with her passengers and mail-bags, to Aden. As we were obliged to haul in pretty close, and were out of compliment obliged to take in our stun-sails, I had a good opportunity of seeing this beautiful vessel, the property of the Honourable East India Company.—Her quarter-deck was crowded by a strange collection of black and white faces of every caste and colour. Servants were running about in their Eastern costumes and overgrown turbans; and under the cabin-windows might be seen—what was a tempting sight to us, who had been so long at sea—nets filled with all sorts of vegetables, fruit, fresh meat, and other good things necessary for the voyage. After a request that she should be reported as soon as we should arrive in Bombay, from whence she had sailed—which request was roared through a speaking-trumpet, by a very little red-faced man, who, by the bye, forgot to ask whether we were in want of water, or had run short of anything—away went the Sesostris, rolling, pitching, and smoking, over the mountain-waves which the late storm had raised up, and which we had happily escaped by one single day.

There appeared to be a singular variety of characters on board of the steamer. I espied two or three jaundiced-looking old men, who, as I supposed, after heaping up riches, and perhaps honours, were tearing themselves away from India, to flutter for a year or two about the sunny side of Cheltenham, and then to die. Others there were, who were pictures of sea-sickness and misery; and in some countenances there was a glow of hope, excited by the thought of once more visiting old England.

Two days after this encounter in the Indian Ocean, we were safely riding at anchor opposite the Fort of Bombay, and in one of the most lovely and picturesque harbours it has been my good fortune to visit. We had been just three months and a half upon our voyage, and I really felt sorry that it was over; for the last ties that seemed still to bind me to sweet home were now to be broken. We had scarcely come to an anchor, before our vessel was surrounded by canoes, punts, dingies, and a dozen different kinds of shore-boats, all of which had come off from the custom-house bunda, in the full expectation of getting a job of some description or other.—One contained the custom-house officers; another, the parties to whom our ship was consigned; another, the master dobie, or ship's washerman, who kindly volunteered to wash for captain, mates, and sailors, at an almost nominal charge. He had a turban full of the highest testimonials, signed by all the known and unknown officers of the Indian army and navy, extending over a period of thirty years, at the very least, and carefully enclosed in an oiled paper envelope. Another boat had been engaged by a collection of Portuguese servant-boys, who were anxious to hire themselves to captain, mate, passengers, or, in fact, to any one that was silly enough to take them on the strength of their suspicious-looking recommendations. Another boat had pulled over a remarkably jolly-looking Hindoo, who kindly offered to dispose, for the commander, of any little thing he might have brought out on his own account to speculate with. He said, in very good English, he was intimately acquainted with all the London and Liverpool ships, and had been the means of putting their captains into the way of realizing large sums on their Yorkshire hams, Cumberland bacon, greyhounds, &c., &c. He was, in fact, a Jew of the St. Mary Axe caste. Another, and perhaps the most acceptable boat in the lot, was filled with all sorts of desirable things; fresh water, new-baked bread, goats' milk, pots of country butter, or ghee, eggs, poultry of all descriptions, meat, vegetables; newspapers, foreign and native; Manilla cheroots, Chinese punkahs, hookahs, pumpkins, and fifty nameless articles, difficult to remember. Then there was a boat crowded with Lascars, fine, strongly-made men, who had come off to assist in unloading the ship; for in warm climates our sailors are unequal to this task without assistance. A knowing-looking Mussulman, seeing me staring about on the quarter-deck, came up the ladder, and after making me a very low and graceful salaam, begged my acceptance of a bunch of sweet green leaves, and a real genuine Provence rose, which appeared to me doubly sweet. He had tied them up neatly on a painted stick; and having thus introduced himself, he began to recommend, in very glowing terms, a young gentleman sitting in the bow of one of the boats, and holding over his head a ragged pink umbrella, as a fit and proper person to look after my luggage, and act as valet de chambre during my sojourn in Bombay. I told him, however, that I should probably have to be my own, for some years to come. He apologised for the intrusion; and was afterwards, with about two dozen others, peremptorily, and rather hastily, ordered off the deck by the mate, as some of the sailors had discovered that our polite visitors had made several mistakes, in taking away with them articles not lawfully their own. No sooner had they pushed off, than it was discovered that the loose ends of every rope had been cut off.—We had evidently fallen amongst thieves, perhaps the most expert and cunning which the world could produce. One of our crew declared that a Lascar was sawing off, with the greatest coolness, and with his hands behind him, about three yards of new rope, as he was conversing with him about the nature of the cargo. It may appear strange, that the captain was not aware of this national failing; but it was his first voyage to India. We got a most acceptable supply of fresh water from the pilot-boat, as we had suffered much during the voyage from the bad tank that ours had been put into. After so long an abstinence, I thought I had never in my life tasted anything so delicious as this water. Truly, we never know the value of any blessing till we lose it.

"And this is India!" thought I, as with a strange feeling of pleasure and surprise, my eyes, as I sate upon a chair on the quarter-deck, wandered over the scenes on shore. "This is the far-famed country concerning which I have heard so much!—the land of gold and sunshine—of nabobs and diamonds; the land of which tradition has told us so many marvellous tales, and of which such wondrous accounts have been handed down, ever since the day when Vasco del Gama, the first European navigator, found his way to India by doubling the Cape of Good Hope; opened, on the 20th of May, 1498, friendly communications with the Zamarin, or Sovereign Prince of Calicut; and laid the foundation of a scheme which was soon to disturb its tranquillity, and to relieve it of a portion of its riches. How little did he dream, that England was eventually to reap the benefits of his discovery, and that a quiet little company of Leadenhall Street merchants would, in due time, take counsel together to turn the trade of Hindostan into a new channel, and to deprive the Venetians, the Genoese, and finally the Portuguese, of all the golden harvest they had been so long reaping on the sunny shores of the famed Indies. Here then was Bombay,* which the Moguls had surrendered up to the Portuguese, in 1530, and which was to be rather more than a century afterwards a part of a wedding-gift of the Infanta of Spain, on her marriage to Charles the Second. My mind pictured

* Bombay takes its name from two Portuguese words, *bom bahia*, signifying a good harbour or bay. It is stated, that in the age of Periplus, this island, then called Kalliena, was little frequented. It had previously been an established port, but Sandanes, one of the Sovereigns of Barugaza, prohibited any of the Egyptian vessels from entering the harbour; and if any were compelled to do so by accident or stress of weather, a guard was immediately put on board, and they were taken to Barugaza.

the fleet of five ships of war, under the command of the Earl of Marlborough, arriving here, in 1662, to take possession of this valuable acquisition, which is now the site of a prosperous and populous city, remarkable for its strong fortifications, magnificent harbour, fine docks, and wealthy merchants; in fact, one of the most flourishing depôts for the produce of the East that we possess. The Island of Bombay is beautifully situated on the western coast of Hindostan, 18 deg. 56 min. N. Lat., and 72 deg. 57 min. E. Long., and lies off the shore of Concan, in the province of Bejapore. It was united, in 1805, to the large and interesting Island of Salsette, on the south, by a noble causeway constructed by the then governor, Mr. Duncan. Bombay is said to be formed of two ranges of whinstone rock, of unequal length, running parallel to each other on opposite sides of the island, and at the distance of two or three miles from each other. The eastern range is about seven, and the western about five miles long; these ranges, being united at the north and south by belts of sandstone, which are only a few feet above the level of the sea. The harbour is bounded on the north and west by Bombay, Colabah, and Salsette. On the eastern side is Butcher's Island; and behind this, Elephanta.—Three miles south of Butcher's Island is Caranjah.—The channel thus formed by Colabah and Caranjah is about three miles wide, and about seven or eight fathom deep; and is rather dangerous, on account of a sunken rock and bank occurring near the entrance to the harbour.

The visitor in Bombay sees, comparatively speaking, but little to gratify his curiosity. Here are no ruined temples, or deserted cities; no jungles, or deserts wild, where lurk the prowling tiger or the savage Thug; and were it not for the exquisite scenery that surrounds it on all sides, this island has in itself but few natural charms to engage our attention, or to merit minute detail. Fort George is the grand resort for foreigners and merchants, and its narrow dingy streets are constantly thronged by crowds from all quarters of the globe. The strange costumes, and odd looking people you are constantly meeting, puzzle you amazingly, before you can find out who they are, or before you can distinguish the different castes of the natives. Here is one man with forty or fifty yards of muslin rolled up into a turban on his head; here another, with a tower of card-board, covered with chintz; there another, with a peak coming down between his eyes, and resting on the bridge of his nose. Then, numbers whom you meet, have peculiar daubs of coloured paint upon their foreheads; caste marks, which are renewed every morning. The light, and cool-looking dresses which all persons wear, thin, long, flowing white robes, and silk or coloured linen trousers, make you quite envy them, and long to cast off your tight, uncomfortable European dress for theirs. There are still a great number of Portuguese here; more, perhaps, than in any other of the presidencies, but they belong chiefly to the poorer classes. They have their churches, chapels, and religious houses; and keep up a great deal of the pomp and outward show of their religion, which is now mixed up with many of the popular superstitions of the Hindoos and Mohammedans. Goa still exists as their gate into India; but this once splendid and populous capital, Mr. Hamilton describes as a wilderness of which the monasteries form the only tenanted portion, and of which a few miserable monks, half of them natives, are the only inhabitants, while whole streets may be traversed, from one extremity to another, without meeting a human being, or any other signs of former population, than pavements overgrown with grass; gardens and court-yards choked with under-wood; and princely dwellings, and venerable abbeys mouldering rapidly into decay. The magnificent churches and monasteries of Goa cannot easily be forgotten by those who have visited this once fearfully celebrated seat of the Inquisition. It is situated 250 miles to the south of Bombay, and few can witness its perishing greatness, without feeling that the hand of an angry God resteth upon it. But Goa still continues to supply India with fresh recruits for the service of the Pope; and sadly did it mourn over the loss of Bombay, and the thought that it was to come into the possession of the vile English heretics. We know that England is accused of injustice towards India, but we cannot say that she has been indifferent to the spiritual welfare and happiness of its countless inhabitants. She has not, like the Romanists, wherever their agents have obtained a footing, pulled down one set of idols to set up another set. The spiritual light which she has poured into India, is the true light of the gospel. The pure, and unadulterated word of God, as preached by those English and American missionaries, who have gone forth to offer to India salvation only through the merits and death of a crucified Redeemer, without money and without price, has been, in a measure, at least, effectual to enlighten its benighted people. It is indeed, but too true, that we have but feebly obeyed the command of our Divine Master, to "Go into all nations, and preach the gospel to every creature." We have not done in this matter, so much as we might have done, and as it was our duty to do. While countless treasures have been drawn from this fair land, to minister to England's national pride, and to subjugate to her power the nations of Southern Asia, how few are the voices which in that vast wilderness of unbelief, are at this present moment preaching forgiveness of sins through the blood of the Redeemer! The harvest truly is plenteous, and has been long ripe for the sickle; but where, it may be asked, are the reapers to gather it in? Here and there indeed, a lone man of God is gloriously expending his health, his strength, his life, in the great cause of man's redemption; but what are these among so many? What provision is this for the spiritual wants of this mighty empire, in which 120,000,000, of our fellow subjects are lost in the thick darkness of the grossest idolatry? It is but as a drop of water in the ocean, a blade of grass in the forest or the jungle. If but the smallest fraction of the gains of England's merchants as a body, were systematically laid aside for this noble object, how great would be the sum annually collected, and how many more labourers might be sent out into the field of India? Shall it be said of us, that we gather where we have not strewn? We have received from India temporal riches; let us give her those which are eternal.

CHAPTER II.

"I THINK I can see the precise and distinguishing marks of national character, more in these nonsensical minutiæ, than in the most important matters of state."

Early Impressions. A Chat with the Reader. Resources of India. Beautiful Scenery. A Tiger; but a stuffed one. My Friend's Bungalow at Colabah. Its Flowers. Principal Buildings in the Fort. A great Fire. Street Architecture. Minah and other Birds in Towns. Kindness to Animals. Little Children and their Pigeons. A Word on Cleanliness. An Idle Hour at Friths. Bad Speculations. George the Fourth's Bedstead. Native Bazaars, and what may be purchased in them. Markets. Extravagant Rivalry. Hindoo Customs. One Man with two sets of Fingers. How to make a Box and inlay it. The Potdars, and Change for a Rupee. Opium Poisoners. The Arabian Rose-water Sellers. Sweet-meat Vendor. Blind Beggars. Parsee Children. Popish Seminary. Mohammedan Temples. Cripple and Lepers. Devotees and Rogues. Cornwallis and his Friends. Bombay Castle, and Dock Yard. Sally Ports and Sepoys, &c.

IN thus taking up my pen, but to jot down some of my stray reminiscences of India, I would endeavour to perpetuate the memory of days passed amidst its peculiar scenes and people. Early impressions, indeed, are not easily eradicated. The memory clings to them with a wonderful tenacity; they fade not from the mind, however roughly we may afterwards be tossed about upon the stormy waves of life. Early happy hours are the "green spots on memory's waste;" and on the recollection of such green spots we all delight to dwell. Life is not altogether a vale of tears and sorrow; the Almighty, in his great goodness, has provided largely for our solace and gratification, if we would only use his gifts aright; but there are those who go grumbling through the world, with their eyes closed to all its fair creations. With such I would not wish to travel.

It is not my intention to discuss or dwell much upon the rise of our magnificent eastern empire; nor upon its progress, since the fortunes of war placed India under the dominion of Great Britain. Celebrated historians have already done justice to this singularly interesting subject; and have laid before the reading public, volumes, teeming with instruction and amusement. As a simple sketcher of common life and every-day scenes in this country, once the land of fable, I will endeavour, as I proceed, to note down the various little peculiarities that struck me as illustrating the character of its inhabitants—a character thought to be but little changed since the death of Nadir Shah, or the destroyer, Timour. The hand of despotism, indeed, now no longer desolates this once oppressed land — robbing a happy, or shedding the blood of a peaceful race, like that of the Hindoo. The Christian banner of England now waves over a large portion of the East Indies. Our protection and assistance were offered, and accepted with a readiness clearly manifesting that the Mohammedan reign of terror was still fresh upon the national memory. As opportunity may offer itself, we will occasionally leave the busy haunts of men, and wander among woods and silent forests; mark the seasons as they roll along; and take a glance at whatever may be interesting to the naturalist, and to all who love and ponder and commune with Nature in her wildest moods. All the treasures which earth offers to man have, as it is well known, been liberally scattered over the face of this double-harvest-bearing clime; which, in consequence, has excited human ambition, and spurred men on to explore it, in its never-failing resources, even from the snowy heights of the wondrous Himalaya range, down to the spicy shores of Cape Comorin. I shall take care to avoid the folly so often committed and complained of—the folly of giving too high a colouring to pictures of domestic life in the East; but of the beauty and the magnificence of its landscapes and scenery, I do not think it possible that language can convey an adequate description. Truth has been said to be at times more startling than fiction; and with good old sober Truth for our guide, my readers and I may, I hope, make our way onwards very agreeably. India is now brought so near us, through the medium of steam, that English readers naturally look for a little more of the minutiæ of Indian life, than they formerly found in the narratives of travellers. It is true, I can hold out no attractive promises of tiger-hunts or daring adventures in the jungle—a species of information which, as I well know, has cast a charm over the works of some writers on Life in India. These subjects, however, having of late entered largely into the descriptive volumes of almost every adventurer who has ever had an opportunity of letting off a percussion-cap in the East, and of startling his friends at home by its effects, have become familiar to the fireside traveller; so leaving the tigers to those who have had the good fortune to meet with so many of them, and who have turned them to such good account, I must candidly confess, strange though it may appear, that I never had the honour of meeting either lion or tiger in my rambles in India, with the exception, indeed, of a stuffed tiger, that occupied a very important position in the bungalow of a kind friend of mine at Colabah, and who glared upon you just as you entered the reception-room. My friend used to stroke down the skin, and to lament, that so noble an animal as the tiger should have become so scarce, as seldom to be met with in western India. I once expressed some little surprise at this remark; for having but just come over to the country, I fancied, that every clump of brushwood sheltered some horrible wild animal of some kind or another, that was always in readiness to pounce upon you unexpectedly. The kind captain, however, informed me that I was about to commence my *griffinage;* and assured me, that I should think very differently before that eventful period should have expired. What a beautiful bungalow, my friend's was! From the road, you looked down a long vista of mogree and scarlet-flowering acacia trees. In front of a large, handsome porch, grew the custard apple and the guava, in clumps, intermingled with the lovely pomegranate, bearing, at one and the same time, the blushing calabash fruit and its wax-like flowers. Shading the dining-room windows was a shrub, about eight feet high, that every morning during the two months of my residence with my friend, was loaded with hundreds of large brilliant yellow blossoms, which attracted around them all the beautiful butterflies in the neighbourhood. The building was octagonal in shape; so that from whatever quarter a stray breeze might come, you could open the Venetian shutters, and admit it at once. But instead of lingering here, we must go back to Fort George, and Bombay; and cast another glance upon its houses and people.

The Fort and Town of Bombay stands principally on a narrow neck of land, at the south-eastern extremity of the island. The fortifications are strong and substantial towards the sea, but are considered weak on the land side. The Mint, Town-Hall, Cathedral, Scotch Church, Dock-Yards, Arsenal, and Custom-House, are handsome buildings, and, by their style of architecture, give an English character to the place, which rather contradicts your English-formed ideas of

Oriental cities. The houses within the Fort were originally built of wood, with verandahs, and roofs covered in with tiles. But, in 1803, a great fire consumed many of them; and as the population was yearly increasing, a number of dwellings were erected on a salt-ground outside, which had been recovered from the sea, and has since grown up into a large, busy town. Upon my first ramble through the streets of Bombay, the houses struck me as being most uncomfortable places to live in. So far as I could judge, they wanted that life about them, if I may use the expression, which we find in our cheerful English residences. There are no glass windows, but their places are supplied by dusty outside shutters. The walls are all coloured or stuccoed, and the houses being three or four stories high in the Fort, throw gloomy but agreeable shadows over the narrow streets. Some of these buildings, inhabited by Hindoos, give an idea of great antiquity, and are very curious in their architecture. Many have great projecting balconies, roofed over, and supported on elaborately carved wooden pillars, the shafts and capitals of which exhibit various odd and fantastic devices, standing out in bold relief, and evidently taken from the Hindoo mythology. The ends of many of the supporting timbers, that project far out from the walls, are ornamented by grotesque figures, in strange, uncouth attitudes, though often representing very faithfully some of the favourite birds, animals, &c., which are held sacred by the natives; these figures being supposed to watch over, as good spirits, those within-doors. Between the legs of an elephant, or a Brahminy bull, it is not unusual to see a jackdaw's or a pigeon's nest, constructed; and sparrows and minahs bring up their young ones undisturbed in the open mouth of a buffalo, or among the folds of a monster serpent. The minah, (*gracula religiosa, Linn.*) I may here observe, has all the characteristics of the English starling about him, though differing in plumage from that well-known bird. The minah is fond of the abodes of man, and you meet with it in every town and village in India. In the streets here it is not unusual to see flocks of birds, so tame as scarcely to move out of your way as you pass, but no one thinks of disturbing them. The children, most unlike our children at home in all their movements and actions, take but little notice of them; indeed they are taught to love and be kind to all God's creatures, and to deprive nothing of the life which they cannot give. The consequence of this part of their education, which arises from the popular belief in the transmigration of souls, and from which, we think, English parents might gather a useful hint, is, that we see here, as it were, perfect harmony existing between man, beast, and bird. The tameness of these birds, as I must confess, was not "shocking to me;" I was delighted to live in a country where cruelty to the inferior animals was almost unknown, and where the beautiful creatures of the great Creator were justly valued, and not shot down for the mere sport of the idle and vicious. A stream of love, too, is thus infused into the infant mind. We see it in childhood, and we see its fruits in manhood; for the domestic hearth of the gentle Hindoo is never so happy as when surrounded by his descendants, even to the second and third generations. In short, nothing but poverty or death ever separates the members of a Hindoo family. Early of a morning, I have seen little children filling the stone troughs, so often met with in Indian villages, with water, to supply the wants of the many animals that pass up and down during the day, in the dry, hot season; and there was something so touching in this innocent office, that I could have kissed the dark little faces that smiled so sweetly on the pigeons and other birds, as they came fearlessly to bathe in the fresh water so kindly supplied for their use. But I love children, and must make my way back to their houses again.

On each side of the principal entrance of a house at Bombay, there is commonly a small Gothic niche for the reception of lamps, which, in the dwellings of the wealthy natives, are lighted every night with a simple bit of cotton-wool, rolled between the fingers, and stuck into a tin-holder, which is sunk in cocoa-nut oil. Some houses have a winding staircase outside, so as to enable you to reach the flat roof without going through the building; or to ascend to an upper story, which perhaps may be occupied by another branch of the family. The rooms are generally large, but very low and badly ventilated; and from the custom of burning sticks in the form of long slender candles, covered with powdered sandal-wood and saltpetre, are redolent of this sickly scented smoke that hangs over everything. Some of the roofs are only tiled in part, and the flat portion is covered with a fine cement called *chunam*, which, when thoroughly dry, becomes very white and polished. Here may often be seen China vases with flowers planted in them, stone seats in great variety, chairs, and couches for the idler or sleeper. These roofs are much resorted to by Hindoo and Parsee ladies, who go up to pray, unseen by the busy world below; for they are supposed to lose *caste* if they appear in public, and are quite shut out from holding any intercourse with strangers; consequently, their lives are passed in great seclusion from the world, and this is the only opportunity which they enjoy of looking occasionally upon the surrounding beauties of their fair country; and of contemplating at night, from their house-tops, the wonders of the starry firmament. Some of the streets are so narrow, that the buildings on each side almost meet at the top; and such streets are, of course, awfully hot, every breath of air being forbidden to enter. It is true, indeed, that the sun cannot annoy or distress those who are walking below; and this is, certainly, so far an advantage over the broad system; but, upon the whole, these confined streets are a great drawback to the health of the Fort and town. The grand end aimed at in the construction of all Indian buildings is, to defend them as much as possible from the immediate influence of the sun's rays; and various are the devices resorted to, to effect this desirable object. The streets, when I first arrived, were suffered to remain in a very offensive state, more particularly in the northern quarter of the Fort, which is densely inhabited by the poorer classes of Mohammedans and Parsees, who were accustomed to cast out, in front of their dwellings, everything that was of no use within; but scavengers are now employed to clear away the pestilential accumulations that impregnated the breath of heaven with every species of abomination. Almost constant fever, dysentery, and cholera, were of course, the result of this horrid and disgraceful state of things, which thus brought along with it its own reward; and taking into consideration the condition of other native towns which it was my lot to visit, we may easily account for the dreadful ravages which these diseases occasion in the East—sweeping off, as they sometimes do, whole populations, in a very brief space of time. As the fortifications rise to a great height, you have not the least chance of enjoying the morning or evening sea-breeze, unless it be from lofty balconies, windows, or the flat roofs already mentioned; consequently, hundreds of persons leave the Fort at stated hours, and assemble in picturesque groups upon the esplanade, the sea-shore, and in other airy haunts, to chat over the past or coming events of the day.

The bazaars here have but few outward attractions, as the native shopkeepers make no show of their goods outside; not having yet learned the English art of ticketing the trumpery in their windows, or of catching the eye with the astounding intelligence that everything within will be sold at an "enormous sacrifice" by the owners. They sit cross-legged on a chair by the door, casting up their accounts, or fanning themselves leisurely with a punkah. If you are in want of any article, they invariably show you, in the first place, the worst specimen of it in their possession, asking you, however, double its value; and not until they see, that you are about to leave the shop, will they produce what you really want. A number of the best shops are kept by Parsees, who are very fond of trading in English and French goods, which they have either consigned to them in the usual way of business, or which they pick up at the large sales, at Frith's auction rooms, in the Fort, which sales generally take place once a month. At these rooms I occasionally spent an idle hour, in looking over the various and beautiful articles which, gathered together from all parts of the commercial world, bad speculations, and over-crowded markets, have caused to fall under the auctioneer's hammer, and which he is often obliged to dispose of at prices that must be ruinous to their owners. Among the many unaccountable and strange things that find their way to this haunt of all bargain-hunters, I particularly remember seeing here a state-bedstead, which was said to have belonged to George the Fourth, as part of the furniture of the Pavilion at Brighton. It had been sent out, in the hope that its costly gilding and ornaments might tempt some of the wealthy natives to purchase it; but I suspect it has never been sold. The adventures of that bedstead, if one could have truthfully investigated them, must have been rather curious. There was a moral conveyed in its history, on the instability of all human greatness. "*Sic transit gloria mundi.*" The bazaars are distinguished by name, as, the Borahs, the China, the Parsee, &c. &c. The Borahs bazaar is occupied by a class of men I shall have occasion, as I proceed in my sketches, to allude to again in the character of travelling hawkers, so I will not particularize them here, though they resemble the second-hand furniture brokers in London, and their shops display the same endless variety of odds and ends, new and old.

The China bazaar is filled with goods manufactured in that industrious country. Here you may purchase the beautiful feather-screens; punkahs of all shapes and sizes; carved ivory-work in chessmen, backgammon-boxes, netting-cases, card-cases; grass-cloth kerchiefs, rich silks and satins, vases, chimney-piece ornaments, and the familiar little cups and saucers, and teapots, so highly valued by china-loving ladies. There are also found here camphor-wood trunks, so useful to preserve furs, clothing, and books, from insects, and in particular from the white ants, so destructive, in this country to this sort of property. In the Parsees you meet with London, French, and American goods, and all those nicknacks which ladies require; besides articles of Bombay workmanship—particularly the richly inlaid work-boxes, desks, and dressing-cases, which are so justly admired by Europeans; kincob, or gold cloth, so much worn by the rich native children; and the rich Indian muslins. There are one or two good markets in the Fort for the sale of butchers' meat, fish, vegetables, and poultry. Oysters are found in great numbers upon the coast, as well as prawns, and other marine delicacies. Everything in the shape of food is very cheap; and, with care, a single man may live most comfortably on £100 a-year. A dreadful system of extravagant rivalry is, however, carried on amongst the residents at Bombay, many of whom are thus led into the wretched folly of living beyond their means. Young officers, cadets, and writers are gradually affected by the prevailing epidemic; and many become so seriously involved in debt and difficulties, as to be unable to leave the country, which has been their ruin, or ever to get out of the clutches of the money-lending natives. Some of the streets in the new town are exclusively inhabited by castes who work at the same trade. In one may be seen the workmen in brass and copper, which department of trade generally embraces the manufacture of cooking-pans, drinking-vessels, tripod-lamps, and such articles of domestic use; for all these things are made of copper or brass in Bombay, and hammered out to the proper size and shape by manual labour. Every poor native carries with him one of these brass drinking-vessels, or *chattees* when he leaves home of a morning. The design of these chattees for holding water, and lifting it out of the tanks, reminded me of the earthen and bronze vases found at Pompeii and Herculaneum. The mode of drinking among the Hindoos is curious. They never allow the vessel to touch their lips, but, holding the head well back, they pour the fluid from a moderate height into the open mouth; and this, practice has enabled them to do, with perfect ease and convenience. For my own part, I never attempted this feat without imminent danger of choking. I was often surprised, that they should drink in this way, as they are usually very cautious about opening their mouths wide, lest the *evil one* should enter. The most ordinary actions of this singular people, are, with them, religious rites; it would be vain to attempt to describe one half of the religious ceremonies which they practise during every waking hour of their lives. In another street or bazaar you see the palanquin builders, common house joiners, and cabinetmakers, and so on. Indeed, if a person felt disposed to extend his knowledge of such arts, he might here obtain cheap lessons in inlaying, carving, gilding, dying, and embroidery, in all their branches.

As the Hindoos invariably follow, as a religious duty, the profession of their forefathers—which profession has been handed down to them, but little changed by modern improvements, from one generation to another,—they have no secrets in their trade. The tools with which they work are few, and extremely simple in their design and construction; and they always sit in the well-known Oriental posture—their feet being educated to assist their hands in almost every labour which they undertake. I have often gained both amusement and instruction, from observing the important offices which Hindoo feet perform. The joiner seizes the plank between the soles of his feet, and there holds it firmly, till he has planed it so as to make it suit his purpose. A Hindoo workman has two sets of fingers, and such a command has he over those of the feet, that he can lift from the ground, and bring towards his hands, almost any articles of a light nature. Practice has given the natives of the East a control which we do not possess over the muscles generally; and the freedom with which their articulations work, surprises the stiff-made European. The hands of the Hindoos are small, and beautifully formed, and there is an easy grace about all their movements. The Chinese, in my opinion, do not surpass the Hindoos in the art of inlaying. In this work they proceed as follows:—they first, with great neatness, make a box of scented sandal-wood, which grows on the Malabar coast, and which is an expensive wood, and sold by weight in Bombay. The pieces, before they are put together, are sawn with a fine instrument, exactly to fit each into its place; as, this wood is so very brittle in

India, it cannot well be planed. Silver hinges and a silver lock are then put on, as steel or iron rusts so as to be unfit for use: even keys here, worn in the pocket, rust. Having so far proceeded in their work, they cut or saw out, from stained pieces of ivory of all colours, a number of minute pieces, in the shape of octagons, triangles, &c.; and nearly an equal number from thin pieces of virgin silver. They then roughly sketch, on the lid and sides of the box, the design intended to be worked; and having everything in readiness, they cover a small portion of the wood with a strong kind of glue, which does not dry quickly; the coloured ivory and silver plates being disposed according to pattern, or as the taste of the workman may direct. So small are some of the pieces, that one hundred, or more, would lie on a square inch: when the work is quite finished, and the glue sufficiently dry, they level the whole with fine glass-paper, and afterwards polish it; the necessary holes in the sandal-wood are pierced by means of a bow-string-pricker, as this hard wood would fly to pieces if pierced in any other way. Equally expert are some of the natives in carving and chasing, in wood and metal, beautiful figures of birds, beasts, and flowers—using a rude little instrument, about two inches long, not unlike a common nail. They carve in ivory but indifferently. The Potdars, or money-changers, take up their position at the corners of the streets, with their little tables before them, ready to transact business at a moment's notice. If you want small change for a rupee, you have often to go or send to the Potdar for it; and if the applicant be a foreigner, he takes pretty good care to deduct three or four *pice* for the accommodation. These men act sometimes in the capacity of pawnbrokers, by lending small sums of money upon the gold and silver ornaments, which all here possess, in a greater or lesser degree; for she must be a wretchedly poor woman indeed, that cannot show a silver bangle or anklet upon the arm or leg. I may observe that these bangles and anklets are the chief ornaments of the Hindoo woman. They are clasped round the arms and ankles in early youth, and never removed. Many of them are soldered on; and instances have occurred in which the parties wearing them have been murdered, or had the limb cut off, with the purpose of gaining possession of these ornaments, so often the only wealth which the poor boast of on their marriage. A silver ring is also commonly worn on the great and second toe; and the nose and ears are pierced for the insertion of similar ornaments. Those who are too poor to purchase silver bangles, &c., wear hoops of coloured glass, ivory, or bone, which make a curious jingling noise as they walk. The money-lenders purchase or exchange all sorts of foreign coin; and for the few sovereigns that I found at the bottom of my purse, upon landing in India, I received in change, from one of these men, eleven rupees each, equal to twenty-two shillings of our money. I was only sorry I had not more sovereigns to turn them into the Company's silver, as I very soon found that money is obtained with as much difficulty at Bombay as in England; and that people work quite as hard for it there as here. The golden expectations of youth are too often disappointed in India. There is no country in which you sooner become acquainted with the sad realities of life. Even in that rich land, man must eat bread by the sweat of his brow.

The Potdar of the street is not a trusty man to deal with; he will impose upon you whenever opportunity offers. A few days before I left Bombay for England, I was rather anxious to bring home with me some of the native ornaments, and gave their weight in rupees for articles, which, I was told, were composed of pure silver. Upon my arrival in England, however, I was much annoyed to find that the rings, bangles, and nose-ornaments, were only tubes of the precious metal, into which lead had been run, to increase their weight. I had, indeed, paid rather dear for my whistle. But I must not condemn all indiscriminately, for there are numbers of highly respectable Shroffs, or native bankers, who have their own private offices in the Fort, and belong to quite a different class from that of our humble friend of the streets; and as the business of banking is chiefly confined, in the interior of India, to the issuing and discounting of bills of exchange, or what are called Hoondies, the Shroff is a most useful man; and from the immense number of these hoondies that are in circulation, we may conclude that petty tradesmen would get on badly without their assistance. Our Potdar of the corner is furnished with an inkstand, pens and paper, acids for testing the genuineness of coin, &c., and generally a pair of old-fashioned spectacles; for the money-changer is generally an old man, and cannot depend implicitly upon his own eyes.

The opium seller has also his little table in the public street, with his box and scales upon it, and tempting samples of the "dreamy drug." One glance at the man will convince you that he is one of his own best customers; the soiled and disorderly turban and dress show you that he is not himself. As a poisoner, who shuns the broad day, he comes creeping out of some narrow, dark alley, just when

> "Morn her rosy steps in the Eastern clime,
> Advancing, sows the earth with orient pearl,"

And man is tempted to stroll abroad early to breathe the cool atmosphere, and gaze upon the landscape still glittering with the dews of night. This is *his* hour for business; for the effects of the last night's dose are worn off, and the wretched victims who surround his table are eager to purchase the day's allowance of the slow, yet sure poison, which he offers, to tranquillize the wandering and disturbed brain of each. Alas! what a fearful group is here: youth, with the sunken eye and languid frame; old age, extreme old age, tottering on two bamboos, in ragged and neglected garments. Each palsied hand scatters down the few *annas* demanded in payment, and then the purchaser, as if he dreaded the detecting eye of his happier and more resolute fellow-creature, skulks feebly back to his home, to enjoy an artificial state of existence, too dearly purchased by a premature and unlamented death, and by the destruction of every natural feeling implanted within him. This fearful species of intoxication is more generally practised among the inhabitants of British India than has been commonly supposed. The Mohammedans in particular are much addicted to its use; and much of the apathy and indifference observable in the native character may be attributed to this universal evil which would seem to be daily gaining ground among them. Few can be surprised that the Emperor of China fought hard to prevent the importation of opium into his dominions by the East India Company. Well might that monarch regard that potent drug as a curse to a nation which had already begun to suffer from its dangerous seduction, and which showed for it a decided taste. East-Indian opium, which is inferior to that of Turkey, is generally grown in Malwa, Bahar, and Benares, the great seat of Brahminical learning. It is stated, that, in Malwa, 360,000 pounds are annually produced, but it is often adulterated with cow dung, decayed leaves, and other filthy impurities. Morewood has calculated that 16,500 pounds annually find their way into Great Britain; but, of course, a large portion of this must be exported to the colonies, as it cannot be consumed as a medicine in such quantities. A few facts, however, which I have been enabled to glean, show that opium-eating is on the increase in our own land, and the following startling account, lately communicated to me, may, perhaps, surprise some of my readers:—"The practice of taking opium, laudanum, ether, and morphia, has increased, and is increasing, amongst the population of the fens in Cambridgeshire and Lincolnshire, to a frightful extent. It prevails amongst the aged, the infirm, and the young; and it is confined to neither sex—old men, old women, and young women, are equally its victims. It may safely be averred, that every second customer who visits the druggists, purchases opium, laudanum, or some opiate or narcotic. It is common to see the man or woman of twenty, thirty, or forty years of age, daily going for his or her sixpenny-worth of poison; and we have heard of yearly bills of £20 in one family, for opium and laudanum. In the town of Wisbeach alone, there are four hundred gallons of laudanum sold and swallowed every year: eight gallons of laudanum per week!

After this revelation, I need not enlarge on East Indian opium-eaters; we will, therefore, turn our attention to the Arabian, who perambulates the streets of Bombay with his country wares and produce. The curious-shaped bottles strung round his neck, are filled with delicious rose-water, of which the Hindoos and Parsees are passionately fond, and which they sprinkle over their apartments and their visitors, as the Roman Catholics do holy water. The Arabian brings over from the Persian Gulf all sorts of coogies, or water-filterers and holders, and his sugar-loaf baskets of plaited grass-weed, strongly made and useful, particularly attract the eye of the English. He deals in costly perfumes, and tempts you to purchase by the scents of otto, or attah, of Persia, in miniature bottles, which he does not fail to recommend in his soft language. He also deals in dates, which are usually packed in round, unglazed jars; they are better and finer than those grown in India, the Arabian method of drying them being superior. The date is perhaps one of the most wholesome fruits we have; and the Arabs half live upon it. His curious straw turban, made like his baskets, distinguishes the Arabian from the crowds around him, and his spare figure and high cheek-bones seldom fail to attract attention. The sweetmeat-vender has his little stall spread out in the street. What a curious collection of things do we find here to tempt the appetite, or to quench the parching thirst of Indian children. Here are rows of brown saucers with lids on, filled with a species of electuary, made out of plantains, sugar, rasped cocoa-nut, and butter; the whole being flavoured with lime-juice—fried peas and grain at a pice a measure, papers of materials for making curry-powder, glasses of toffy, heaps of fruits, jars of fresh toddy, betal-nut, and cakes decked out with scraps of tinsel, slices of melons, pumpkins, cucumbers, and green sugar-cane, with nameless preserves that are imported from China in sealed packages.

But who are these men whom we see in a long string of ten or a dozen, holding by the skirts of each other's robes, and each a staff in his right hand, all led by a little boy, who guides them? They are the wandering, blind beggars of the land; the victims of amaurosis, a disease which is generally brought on by too great exposure to the heat and glare of the sun. Poor creatures! we do indeed feel for you! Oh! that we had the power to touch those sightless orbs with healing ointment, and give them sight once more. How touching is that voice of supplication, asking for the smallest sum, the least relief! What was Milton's blindness compared to thine, who hast to travel over burning wastes, and dreary lands, to beg thy daily pittance? What sweet and placid resignation do I see in that countenance! But He who has thought fit to afflict thee, has implanted in the breasts of thy fellow-creatures, that most excellent gift of charity; and the poor Hindoo drops his mite into thy trembling hand, as he hurries past upon his way. And is there no home in this mighty empire where thy aged limbs may rest, before death summons' thee away?

We will dwell no longer upon this painful picture that casts a shadow on our path, but will turn to those happy children that come laughing onward in their little lilliputian coach, drawn by four beautiful goats, with long ears and silky coats. They are going to take their evening drive, in charge of two servants. The one who walks behind, holds over them a splendid crimson, China-satin chittree, with a gold fringe of chaste design, as large as our gig umbrellas; and he who leads the animals is an old and faithful domestic of the Parsee family, to whom they belong. Let us examine the costume of these loved ones; for loved they must be, if we may judge by the care and taste displayed in the arrangement of the luxuriant curls that hang down the back of each boy. They all wear flowered, white muslin tunics, full in the sleeves, gathered up in folds round the wrist, and fitting tight round the neck and waist. Under this almost transparent robe, may be detected a yellow satin boddice, also fitting tight; and then we come to the full Turkish silk trousers, with white socks, and embroidered slippers; skull-caps of kincob, and a costly pearl or emerald in each ear, complete the dress of the children of the Parsee gentleman; and what happy little round faces they exhibit! you see at once, that they are the children of wealthy parents, as the sun has been carefully shaded away from them, and a pleasing tinge on the cheek just tells of their own sunny clime. But they have passed over the drawbridge, and under the old gateway that leads out of the fort, and the sepoy on duty recommences his walk, which had been arrested for the moment, as these little birds-of-paradise flew past him to sport amid the flower gardens of Bycullah; he had, perhaps, seen them every evening; but we never tire of looking on beautiful children—little angels are they, that are permitted to flit around us to give us an idea of heaven, for of such is that kingdom.

There is a dark, monastic-looking building near us, enclosed by high walls, and shaded by a few towering palm-trees that grow out of the court-yard. Just an hour ago the vesper-bell might have been heard calling its inmates to prayers, for it is a Romish Portuguese seminary, for the education of youth destined for the church; and though the pupils are tall, full-grown young men, they may be seen coming out two-and-two into the esplanade like schoolboys parading for a walk. They all wear black, short gowns, with white collars turned over the shoulders, a kind of Oxford cap, and buckles in their shoes. The robust well-fed looking men, who in puce surplices and bishops' hats, walking on each side, are the priests connected with this establishment. One of the members of this seminary told me, their priests will never allow them to read an English bible, on the plea that it is not faithfully translated. I fear the translation which they do read, has not tended much to improve their morals, if we may judge from their daily walk and conduct. The natives unfortunately judge *our* religion by theirs, at least, some with whom I have conversed could not clearly comprehend the practical difference between corrupted Popery and Protestantism, seeing that we all, as they said, called ourselves Christians.

The entrance to all the Mohammedan and Hindoo temples and pagodas are beset with beggars of every description, who keep up a perpetual baying all day long, soliciting charity and alms from those who go in to pray, or are passing in the streets. Here, the cripple is put down by his friend upon a mat in a shaded place, early in the morning, to excite the compassion of the multitude. Some of these poor creatures are so frightfully deformed, as to make you turn away almost involuntarily from the hideous lump of disease spread out before you. I have seen at these places some very curious and novel distortions of the vertebræ, and remember particularly one man, whom I often stayed to look at, and whose head was completely reversed, the chin apparently resting a little below the nape of the neck. The afflicted leper stands here with his arms and legs fully exposed; they look as if they had been covered with old white-wash, which was scaling off from the dark ground underneath; but he stands alone, and his companions in misery shun his neighbourhood as contagious. Some of these men are cripples by nature, and some by art, and very many are arrant knaves and impostors. Sunyasse Brahmins; Faquirs, and other religious devotees, contrive to obtain a very good livelihood at these temples, and along the road sides and often startle you with their painted bodies, and idiotic expression of countenance. Such various and interesting descriptions have been given of these people, that I have scarcely anything fresh to offer on the subject. But I would not, indeed, be understood to insinuate, that all who are met with in India in the character of religious devotees, are impostors. Many of them have been known to suffer, by way of expiation for their crimes, the greatest self-imposed tortures; trusting, that by a life of present misery they might, when death should arrive, be carried on angels' wings to dwell for ever in happiness with the houris of paradise. Sitting between two fires till half roasted—swinging from a tree by a hook through the back—pushing before them as the Mohammedans will do for hundreds of miles across a country down to the sea a little cart, on their hands and knees, in their pilgrimage to Mecca—and holding a flower-pot in the hand, as a man does, in a sort of sacred enclosure or garden near to Bombay, till the roots have grown through the back of it, and his nails are like the talons of a bird; these and other such vain and useless penances are too well attested to require any confirmation from me. Many such deeds I have myself witnessed; for the stranger, upon landing in Bombay, generally takes an early opportunity of seeing some of these poor deluded creatures, who are to be met with in its vicinity.

In the centre of a large railed enclosure in the Fort, there is a very handsome monument erected to the Marquis of Cornwallis, who superseded the celebrated Warren Hastings in the office of governor-general of India. You seldom pass it without seeing groups of people lounging about it, or sitting on the steps leading up to it; and the natives are very fond of throwing in under the dome, that protects the figure, flowers, and bits of coloured paper, and these have gradually accumulated in such heaps as almost to conceal two melancholy marble ladies, who are gazing sweetly on the besieger of Seringapatam. Upon making some enquiries, I learned, that these flowers, &c., were thrown in as offerings, and that the hero had been made an idol of by some of the Mohammedans—but this is not correct; they only resort hither to pray, because it is a quiet and retired place, and the poor Parsee has a better view from this elevated position of the rising sun. The town-hall forms one side of this square, and is certainly a very elegant building. At one end of it is the news-room and library, which contains some curious Hindoo deities, and other relics of Indian antiquity. A branch of the Royal Asiatic Society here holds its meetings. Close to the town-hall is an enormous circular tank, capable of supplying the whole garrison, and those who reside within the walls, with water, in case of any popular outbreak; and about two hundred yards, and overlooking the harbour, is Bombay Castle, a strong substantial building, swarming with sepoys and officers. The Green, as this square is called, is prettily planted with rows of trees; and the old government-house, now turned into a secretariate, cathedral, and mint, stand near it.

The dock-yard at Bombay is always a very busy

scene, as the East India Company build all their steam and war-ships there, and numbers of the native labourers are employed in their construction; they are superintended by Scotch or English engineers, and, with the aid of their instructions, the machinery of these vessels, intended chiefly for the Indian navy, is there made and put together; formerly, it was sent out in a finished state, and of course at a great expense. As the harbour of Bombay is thought to be unequalled in British India, and so favourably situated for commerce, with the advantage of its deep tide-water, most excellent docks have been constructed for the accommodation of shipping. The forests of Malabar supply them with abundance of the finest teak timber for building purposes. There are three principal entrances into the Fort; fine, handsome, military-looking gateways, with guard-houses erected over their arches, and three or four sally-ports between them, that run under the massive fortifica tions, and cross the wet moat by a narrow foot-bridge. A strong embankment outside slopes down to the esplanade. They are all closed at nine o'clock, every evening, and opened at gun-fire (day-light), in the morning. Sentries are on guard here, night and day. Bombay has long been the nursery for our native sailors and soldiers; and the sepoy is proud of the rank which he sustains in our armies of the East; but neither he nor his superior officers can entirely give up old customs and habits; and when the duties of parade are over, and they return to their barracks, you will commonly find them squatted in the centre of the room, eating their rice and curry out of chattees. Their pay is less than that of the English soldier, but their wants are fewer in comparison. No one can find fault with this arrangement, when we consider what our countrymen have often to suffer in this burning climate, banished as they are, for a period of *twenty-one* years, from their own happy land.—How few, how very few are those who live to return with the regiment with which they went out! 'Tis true, we hear of such and such companies arriving at Chatham and elsewhere, from India, in good health, after that length of absence; but how many of those who originally composed it are to be found in its ranks? Yet, these circumstances do not appear to daunt the British soldier. He knows his pay will be good in India, and that, with care, he may lay by a little, every year, for old age, should it please Providence to prolong his life; for the Honourable East India Company are noble pay-masters to all their servants; and we often find in their employ many of England's bravest sons. I have heard it stated, that every soldier sent out to India costs the government £25 for the voyage alone. This enormous expense, with £90 allowed to every officer, may account for the length of the period during which they are required to remain in India.

Camels, buffaloes, and other large native animals, are not permitted to be led through the streets of Bombay, as they startle the horses; but groups of them are met with outside on the esplanade, and give a truly Eastern character to the scene. I shall, however, have occasion to allude again to this gay place, as it appears in the hot season, when every stranger and resident able to command a buggy, turns out for an hour or two's drive before dinner.

There are two or three good weekly papers published in Bombay, and the same number in the Hindoostannee language. The art of printing has made great advance here, particularly the lithographic branch, which is well adapted to Eastern languages. But it is to be lamented, that Christians should use this valuable gift, for the dissemination of such works as the Koran, &c. Since I left Bombay, an Indian paper informs me, that 15,000 copies of this work have been lately worked off and sold at two rupees a copy. Formerly, the Koran could not be purchased for less than twenty or thirty rupees.

CHAPTER III.

"Two tyrant-seasons rule the wide domain,
Scorch with dry heat, or drench with floods of rain:
Now feverish herds rush maddening o'er the plains
And cool in shady streams their throbbing veins;
The birds drop lifeless from the silent spray,
And Nature faints beneath the fiery day:
Then bursts the deluge on the sinking shore,
And teeming Plenty opens all her store."

Climates. South-west Monsoon. Mango Showers. Put your house in Order. Letters and Post Men. Palanquins. Clearing Tents off the Esplanade. Warm Clothing. Why I was called a Griffin. The Rains at last descend. Atmospheric changes. Appearance of the ocean. Awful thunder and lightning. Nature is agitated. The Sun darkened. Strife of the elements. Tempest terrific to behold. Houses shaken in the Fort. The floods. Scene pregnant with horrors. Flying Bugs and hideous Spiders. A Rest for the Punkahs. What the Poor Natives suffer at this Season. A Glance from our Bungalow. Wonderful changes in the Vegetable World. Flowers and Fruits. Golden Oriole and Jungle Cock. Shere Khan and his Good Works. Neglect of Old Tanks. Cool Breezes and Delhi Shawls. A Peep into the Sick Man's Chamber. Jellies and Sweet Peas. How to eat Mangoes. Poisonous Miasma. Hindoo Festival of Cocoa-nut-Day. Offerings to the Ocean. Farewell to the Rains, &c., &c.

THOSE who are familiar only with the climate of England, with its sunshine and its storms; and with the wild aspect of its long dreary winters, when the northern districts of our island put on so early their mantle of snow, and rivers and lakes, locked up in their icy prisons, are bound together for weeks by an invisible hand—those who are accustomed to the regular variations of temperature, which, notwithstanding the frequent and sudden changes which we experience from heat to cold, give an almost decided character to the four seasons that sum up our year, can form but an imperfect idea of other lands, where the sun, for eight months out of the twelve, is scarcely shadowed by a cloud, and where frost and snow are almost unknown. Nature is boundless in her resources; and the more we inquire and examine, the more we are lost in wonder and admiration at the great scheme for carrying on so beautifully the designs of the Creator, so that seed time and harvest, summer and winter, shall still be given to man, and God's promises stand fast for ever. Though some districts of India are often left nine months together without rain, yet an ample provision has been made to counteract the ill effects of so long a drought upon a country so much exposed to a burning sun. Vegetation, which with us would speedily perish without an abundant supply of rain, is there sufficiently nourished by that moisture which plants, as they bud and blossom, and produce their fruit, have the power of hoarding up and retaining from one rainy season to another, and by the heavy dews that nightly fall upon their large, expanded leaves. Those remarkable periodical rains, commonly called the south-west Monsoons, generally set in at Bombay about the month of May, and terminate at the close of August. Three weeks or a month before their commencement, some light precursory showers pass over the land, but they eldom continue more than a day or two, and are suceeded by the usual hot and clear weather. Occasionally the preparatory fall is accompanied by thunder and lightning; but this is not an invariable rule. These preparatory rains are called "mangoe showers;" the natives, who have given them this appellation, believing that that delicious fruit, the mangoe, the boast of this part of India, could not come to perfection without them. How far this opinion may be correct, I know not; but certain it is, that the mangoe begins to ripen at this particular period of the year, and to acquire that rich yellow tinge, which makes it so conspicuous on the tree. To man, these showers act as a warning to set his house in order; for we cannot tell how soon the storm may arise, that must ere long burst upon him, with dreadful fury.—Consequently, all persons, at this season of the year, are busy tarring, painting, and repairing the tiles, or thatch, forming the covering of their houses; and making all secure, and impervious to the coming rains. The sewers in the streets, and other water-courses, are examined and put into good order, and the large artificial tanks, from which the inhabitants look anxiously for their eight months' supply of water, are fresh cemented and carefully repaired. Tents are now taken down, and the temporary abodes erected on the esplanade, sea-shore, and other cool situations, are speedily cleared off the ground, and stored away in warehouses in the Fort, until the return of the settled weather. The merchant now thinks it necessary to enclose all his country despatches in oiled or waxed paper cases, as he is aware that the rivers will soon be flooded, and that the Tapall must swim over with the post-bags on his head. In the cocoa-nut and date plantations, the old toddy-drawers are very busy collecting all the large spreading leaves that have fallen and been stripped from these valuable trees for the purpose of covering in verandahs, sheds for cattle, and rain-dresses for the poorer class of natives. Shegrams, buggies, and bullock hackery conveyances have their sun-shades taken off, and varnished coverings put on; and all palanquins are carefully examined, and their cracks filled up with putty or chunam.—Those who can afford glass windows in their bungalows have them now put in, to supply the place of the common open Venetian blinds; and the large monument on the esplanade, erected to the memory of the Marquis of Wellesley, is enclosed by a huge wooden box built around the iron railings that protect it; to be no more stared at by the Portuguese, or criticised by the modern arrivals from England, until the rains are over. Officers commanding regiments at outstations, who have been expecting for months to receive the welcome orders from head-quarters to march, have now ceased to hope for any change till after October, or the beginning of November. The bazaars display a great variety of China; also of French, English, and native leaf chittrees or umbrellas; and the making up of flannel and other warm clothing for the European part of the population, affords abnndant employment to the Dergees.—American boots and shoes have great sale; for those manufactured in the country, though very neat, and well adapted for dry weather, will not stand wet; the tanning of the leather is bad, and the first few showers separate the soles from the upper leather. Not being aware of this circumstance, I was one day deprived of the heel of my boot when out walking; and I was heartily laughed at on my return home, and immediately set down as a "Griffin," a term commonly applied to those who have not passed twelve months in the country, and gone through the usual amount of Indian troubles and annoyances. The day at length arrives when the windows of heaven are to be opened, and man's anxious doubts and fears are to be dispelled by this gracious provision for his wants. Dark clouds, towards noon, gather in the south-west, and gradually steal over the azure firmament, casting a gloomy shadow upon the earth, and obscuring the intensity of the sun's rays, as they flit over his surface in their onward progress. A current of cool, strange air now denotes some remarkable atmospheric change. The ocean is unusually agitated; the waves are lifted up—hurried onwards as the breeze increases—the angry waters come foaming and roaring towards the shore, and are broken with violence upon the rocks; receding but to break again with redoubled force.—Distant peals of thunder echo among the lofty ghauts far down the coast, and vivid streams of forked lightning illumine their peaked summits. The dry leaves of the lofty palms rattle overhead, and the forests are agitated and shaken as the hurricane roars through their solemn vistas, and breaks in upon their profound stillness. The soaring kite flaps his outstretched wings, as he rises alarmed from his lone perch, and is hurried away upon the storm. The cattle on the plains congregate together, as if driven by some irresistible impulse to seek the shelter and protection of each other, and lie down with their heads close to the earth, as if conscious of approaching danger; and the poor Hindoo wraps his muslin *kummerband* tighter around him, as the cool air expands its many folds, and exposes his delicately-formed limbs to the chilly blast. The skies become darkened, and sheets of blazing lightning, followed up by the roar of deafening thunder, succeed each other with fearful rapidity; and, though in broad day, the eye can scarcely bear to look upon the flaming heavens, so intense is their brightness. The elements are indeed at war. Large drops of rain begin to fall; and falling, raise up, in consequence of their weight, a cloud of dust; and then, within a brief space, the mighty floods descend upon the thirsty land. The tempest is terrific to behold, and man trembles beneath the storm. He seeks in haste the shelter of his mud-built cabin, and mutters a hurried prayer tó the stone idol which he has set up. The high houses in the Fort of Bombay vibrate with every clap of thunder; doors and windows, and walls and floors are shaken by the loud artillery of heaven. Torrents of water pour down from every roof, and bound over, in broken streams, the sounding verandahs below them, sweeping the various streets as the flood rushes onward, laden with mud and rubbish, towards the sea. To those persons who have but just arrived in the country, and who, having never experienced the setting in of this remarkable season, have formed from description but an imperfect idea of that change, the scene is pregnant with horror of every kind. The newly-arrived English woman in particular suffers exceedingly at this period, being scarcely able to divest herself of the impression, that everything around her is about to be destroyed or washed away; yet it is very seldom that accidents occur, or that property is seriously injured. Occasionally we hear of exposed houses being struck by lightning on the island, of old palm trees blown down, and of leaf roofs being dispersed to the four winds of heaven; for woe be unto him who lives in a bungalow with a bad roof, or in one whose spouts are out of order: but with these exceptions, Europeans on shore have but little to be alarmed about for their personal safety. Myriads of mosquitoes, now driven in by the rains, fill your apartments; and your lamps at night, if not properly covered over with a glass shade, are liable to be suddenly extinguished by the large green beetles that have sought shelter from the storm without. Flying bugs almost poison you with their fœtid effluvia, and contaminate every article of food upon which they may chance to alight. The musk-weasels dart in under your China matting, and find their way into your wine-cellars, and every cork they touch, every bottle they spoil. That nimble and really useful reptile, the house lizard, climbs your walls in all directions, and comes out so regularly from under your table after dinner, to feed upon the flies attracted thither, that you quite look for the active little creature as a matter of course, to amuse you during dessert time; and if he fail to appear, express regret, as I have heard an old gentleman do, at its non-arrival. The loathsome centipede gets into your cooking-houses, and hideous spiders, with hairy bodies and long legs, take up their quarters in every available corner and door-way. They are not content with staying at home quietly like our own respectable, though small species, and of taking their chance of what may be sent them; but they must make daily tours all over the establishment, as if it were expected, that they should pay visits to one another, now that the season had brought them into town. In fact, all the entomological tormentors of India appear to have a design upon your house and happiness. A continual buzzing is kept up around you day and night. Ants creep up your legs, while fleas irritate your body; and farewell to sleep, if your gauze curtains display any rents at bed-time. The punkahs or swinging fans, suspended in your rooms, now have rest from their labours, for the atmosphere is sufficiently cool without any artificial currents of air. The sweet-scented cuscus-mats, or tatties, hung outside between the pillars that support your verandah, and kept wet, in order to lower the temperature of the heated breeze before it enters your house, are now taken down and laid aside; and quite a change takes place in all your little plans within doors. The poor thinly-clad labourers are dreadfully susceptible of cold now; and instead of welcoming the monsoons as a providential visitation ordained by the Almighty for their especial good, they grumble at their long continuance, and rejoice at their departure. 'Tis true the natives suffer much at this inclement season from fever and ague; and the hummals or palanquin bearers, who are necessitated to be out constantly in the rains while carrying their employers to the various scenes of their daily duties, are much to be pitied, as they are liable to attacks of rheumatic fever, and often fall victims to dysentery and cholera in a few hours. These persons are such strange figures, and are dressed up in such odd garments, with their heads and faces tied up to protect them from the weather, that it is difficult to decide to what caste or country they belong. As a class of labourers, they often excited my compassion, as I must say with our good queen Elizabeth, that it is degrading to see men groaning under the weight of their idle fellow-creatures; and in India these poor wretches have to endure much from direct exposure to the sun, as they cannot, when bearing a palanquin, carry any chittree to shield them from its dangerous heat. I never felt comfortable in one of these palanquins, and hope some humane governor will endeavour to do away with this fashionable mode of conveyance; and that the poor hummals, so long neglected, may rise a little in the scale of civilization. I have seen them deposit their human burdens, after a long journey, perhaps, of four or five miles in the hot season, and sink down almost exhausted upon the door-step, bathed in profuse perspiration that poured down from their panting bodies; and often, on such occasions, have I thought of the comparatively luxurious lives led by our hackney-coachmen. You hire these men by the day, week, or month; but if you keep your own palanquin, they are considered as a part of your domestic establishment, and reside in the compound, or somewhere close to your residence. Palanquins are close and uncomfortable affairs, and, moreover, are extremely awkward to get into, or out of. They are something resembling a sedan-chair turned over upon its side, with a pole sticking out at each end; which pole, when elevated, rests upon the shoulders of the bearers. While carrying them, the hummals have often to rest and change sides, as the swinging motion of the machine soon injures the shoulder, though well protected by a soft woollen pad. How any man can call it a luxury to be carried about the country in one of these close boxes, at the expense of so much seeming suffering to his fellow-creatures, I cannot conceive.

We will now steal out from our bungalow, caring little for the pelting storm, for we shall keep under the magnificent plantain leaves that hang over the foot-path, and take a peep at the face of nature—at the fields and woods; and see the wondrous change which a few days' rain has produced in the vegetable world.

> "But who can paint
> Like Nature? can imagination boast
> Amidst its gay creation, hues like hers?
> And lay them on so delicately fine,
> And lose them in each other, as appears
> In every bud that blows? If fancy then,
> Unequal, fail beneath the pleasing task,
> Ah! what shall language do?"

The dry and burnt up plain that crackled under our feet like the stubble of harvest, is now covered with fine grass a foot deep, and of that rich emerald green, which is so refreshing to the eye, and so novel in its appearance, that you feel transplanted, as it were, to some strange land, or to the waving meadows of England's Spring. The united influence of heat and moisture are at work. Every tree and shrub has sent forth some new leaves or tender shoots, and the gums which so long protected them are now dissolved, and diffuse a delicious perfume around you. The cool rains and mild temperature at this season, produce a luxuriance of vegetation unknown, perhaps, in any other country on the face of the earth. The extraordinary and rapid growth of all seeds now planted, appears more like the work of enchantment, than the usual slow progress of nature familiar to us in our northern latitudes. The gourd, melon, and cucumber, have now gained the roof of the peasant's hut, and promise by their shining blossoms a plentiful supply of their cooling fruits when the hot season shall arrive. Trees and plants, that during the dry months, had shut up all their pores, so as not to be robbed of their juices by evaporation; and roots, that lay buried in the deep sands, or strong clay districts, now spring suddenly into life and beauty, in places that were before barren to the eye. Creeping plants, that run along the ground, now embrace the trunks of trees, and ascend them with astonishing rapidity, running out upon their branches, and so travelling from one to another, till the forests in the neighbourhood of Bombay appear to be bound together, and canopied over, by the thousand lovely climbers that cast an almost night-like gloom on all things below them. From some of these branches may be seen the charming blossoms of the convolvulus, and other flowering parasitical plants, floating between heaven and earth in graceful festoons, uninjured by the floods of rain, and affording support to all those delicate birds and insects that would perish without this beautiful provision of the great Author of Nature. The woods are now alive with the feathered tribes, and the soft cooing of the turtle-dove, a bird held sacred in India, is repeated for miles around you. The golden oriole, and the azure jay, descending from the lofty trees, now feast upon the luscious fruits; and our own English barn-door bird, the stately jungle cock, makes the coverts ring again with his loud and familiar note, as he sweeps through the sounding woods, and is lost in their deep shadows. We must now turn aside from these pleasing pictures of the Indian forest, at which we have but glanced hurriedly. Memory fails me in recalling the many beauties that surround us here on all sides, and the abundant supply of food that the fields promise to man. The sea, formerly so transparent and serene, is now discoloured by the large rivers, that carry down enormous quantities of earth in their swift and destructive progress. All coasting traffic ceases; and the cocoa-nut sewn Pattemars, and fishing dingie have sought the shelter of some friendly creek or land-locked bay, for three months at least. The Company's steamers change the time of their going to Aden, and the Persian Gulf with the overland mails; and whereas a very brief delay would, at any other time, cause alarm, a weeks' detention now beyond their time, is scarcely spoken of with surprise, as every one is aware that the monsoons are the cause. Internal communication is now almost laid aside, and no person, who can possibly avoid it, travels either by land or water. The mail-bags,* usually forwarded by runners, each a stage of three coss, or six miles, are often detained for weeks, before an opportunity occurs to ford or swim over the swollen rivers and nullahs! a work often of much difficulty and danger. Weekly reports of heart-rending shipwrecks fill the native papers, and a catalogue of flooded districts, and other disasters from the country, too often give a painful interest to the rainy season. Yet we must not lose sight of the goodness of the Almighty, in sending these blessed showers at stated periods; for, were they but once withheld, the most dreadful consequences must ensue, and thousands upon thousands of human creatures would perish for want of water. We are helped to form some little idea of the value of that necessary article, when we see scattered over India the enormous public and private tanks, which at the rainy season must be replenished, to meet the demands of a large population like that of India, and which have been erected at a

* The Bombay Times thus describes the present bad management (1849) of the Post office in Gangetic India. "Newspapers are charged by weight, so that before they can pass for single postage, they must make use of the smallest-sized sheet to be found in the meanest provincial town in England; the paper must be as thin as a bank note. In our rainy season, if near full weight, it absorbs moisture so rapidly, as to be charged double postage at its journey's end; the postage on a daily paper from moderate distances amounts to £5. a-year; the mails are carried in leather bags on men's heads, and so negligently made up, that they occasionally reach their destination in a state of pulp. Thousands of rupees are annually abstracted from letters, and every variety of misconduct prevails."

vast expense. Its successive rulers never neglected this all-important duty; and the building of tanks, long before the Mohammedan invasion, was a common act of charity among the Hindoo rajahs, who thus handed their names down to posterity, and enriched the districts in which they resided. Shere Khan, a Patan chief, set a noble example to others. He formed a high road across the entire breadth of Hindostan, from the Ganges to the Indus, along which he caused fruit trees to be planted; a well to be sunk every two miles, and a caravansera to be provided at every stage, so that travellers might be accommodated at the public expense. Ferose the Third, who is said to have built during his reign, a hundred bridges, forty mosques, and thirty colleges, with many other works of utility; also erected thirty reservoirs for the purposes of irrigation, and the general good of the country. Some of these tanks, which have now, through the bad policy of the East India Company, been allowed to fall into a sad state of decay, are still very handsome and remarkable buildings. One which I saw in Guzerat, cost originally, as I was told, nine lacks of rupees in its construction! and even in the dry season, it contained an abundant supply of the coolest and purest water. I recollect being surprised, upon descending the long flight of steps that led to it, to see the place swarming with the large bull-frog, and with a curious species of little tortoise; these creatures, as I was informed by those who went down to draw the water, were fostered and preserved, as they contributed to ensure the purity of the water, by keeping it continually in motion. A wealthy native, who had perhaps committed some dreadful crime, and who on his death-bed had repented, would often will away a large sum of money, to be expended in a particular district where water was scarce, in a public tank. Many have been built under these circumstances, even during the lifetime of the unhappy individual, who well knew this to be the greatest boon that could be conferred upon an agricultural people. Every town and village has its tank; many boast of three or four, and the large capitals are generally well supplied with draw-wells and natural reservoirs in their neighbourhood, which by their presence often assure the wearied, foot-sore traveller, that his journey is drawing to a close. In Bombay, the pluvia-meter is watched in the rainy season with much anxiety; and the quantity of water that falls, in and about that island, is satisfactorily ascertained.

The change that takes place during the continuance of the south-west monsoons, from a temperature of 100 or 120 deg., to one of 65 or 70, is truly delightful to the European; for the air is now cool and delicious, resembling the close of an English spring. Woollen clothing may now be worn with comfort; and ladies wrap themselves up in their large Cashmere shawls and Delhi scarfs, and enjoy the bracing and invigorating breeze. Your sleep is sweet and refreshing, and you rise in the morning with an energy and life unknown in the hot months; and though females cannot take much exercise out of doors, yet they suffer not from confinement, as a hundred little occupations now engage their attention, that could not be pursued with any degree of pleasure before. The lounging-couch is deserted, and the Anglo-Indian lady is once more acting in the capacity of an industrious housewife.

To carry out our reminiscences of this eventful division of the Indian year, we will gently draw aside the silken screen that closes the entrance to that still chamber, where only the voice of pain and passive suffering is occasionally heard to break in upon the death-like silence. The musshall has placed upon the floor the hand-punkah, which is torn and broken by constant use through restless nights and burning days. He thinks that massa can do without it now. A bunch of roses and white mogree blossoms engages the sufferer's attention, and he shakes upon his face, moist with the dews of approaching death, a grateful shower of bright little globules, that rest on the hollows of his cheeks. They are Nature's tears. His long, thin fingers untie the slender cord that binds these cherished flowers together, and a half-expanded rose, still drooping with the rains, is raised to the lips now trembling with emotion. Beautiful flower! what visions of the past dost thou conjure up!—green fields, bubbling fountains, shady woods, and refreshing and balmy gales; and the oft-traversed scenes of early childhood pass by in quick review before the dying man. The flower falls from his hand; the little globules are united to bitter tears, that course their way down his sunken cheeks; and an agony of grief disturbs the swarthy attendant of the sick chamber, who has stolen an hour's sleep upon the matting at the foot of the bed. Yet this is a blessed season for the poor English invalid. After weeks, perhaps months of confinement to the bed of sickness, in a close and heated room, where neither day nor night has brought relief, he offers a thankful acknowledgment to Him from whom proceedeth every good and perfect gift, for the cool breeze that steals through his lattice, and once more fans his feverish and burning brow. Hope, that seemed, so far as he was concerned, to have bid the world farewell, again returns. Home, with its sweet endearments, rushes upon the wandering memory, and his thoughts turn to that far distant land, which he will never see again. The expiring spark of life still burns, and is fanned by the reviving breeze; and the death-stricken invalid talks of a thousand things which he will do when he shall be a little stronger. He feels certain that he must now recover; and he longs to be carried down in his palanquin to the shore, to see riding at anchor those English vessels, one of which, he hopes, is to bear him away from the Indian land; but he will see his distant home no more. A change has, indeed, "come o'er the spirit of his dream."

Instead of pampering the taste, and tempting it with curries and omelets, and other made dishes, you have now a natural appetite. Your water and wine require no artificial cooling; and the ladies pride themselves on the firmness of their jellies, and the durability of their *blanc mange*. Your butchers' meat will keep longer uncooked, and you may even calculate upon seeing your saddle of kid a second time upon your table, cold. Butter ceases to melt when out of water, and custards manufactured in the morning do credit to the cook at supper time. It is pleasing to see boxes of mignionette, sweet peas, and pots of roses flourishing in the verandah. Even apple trees and gooseberries are cherished in this country as great rarities, and are tended with the fondest care, because they speak of happy England, and of all the fond affections and associations of the heart when it was light and young. Indeed, you can almost discover the residences of our fair countrywomen by these little mementoes of their early home. Few can form an idea how high a value is set upon these trifles in a foreign land. Long may the exiled daughters of Britain cherish these sweet feelings, nor allow the transitory pleasures of an Eastern life, however attractive or brilliant, to wean their hearts away from the land of their birth! Now, too, you look forward to a great variety of vegetables at your table. The common and sweet potatoes, yams, turnips, and carrots; the beautiful egg-plant; tomatoes, green-chillies, and ginger, and many others, are to be purchased in the native markets; and delicious fruits abound everywhere; the water and musk melons, cut in slices, are hawked about the streets in large baskets, and your servants are devouring cucumbers, white onions, and new sugar-cane, all day long. Your gardens are almost closed up with flowery shrubs, and the air is scented with the jasmine and powerful tube-rose. And now comes the long looked for mangoe feast, fresh and luscious from the famed plantations near Mazagaon. The guests being seated round a table, each with a long napkin tucked under his chin, and his coat-sleeves turned up to the elbows a large basketful of the fruit is placed in the centre of the board, and you are soon almost suffocated with the powerful aroma that pervades the apartment.—The number of mangoes that a practised person may eat with impunity, is really astonishing. A little pale brandy is taken afterwards, by way of security, and a bath to get rid of the jaundiced complexion is sometimes absolutely necessary. A delicious pickle is made from the fruit before it is quite ripe; and it enters very largely into the composition of chutnee, a curious mixture much used in curries and Indian made dishes. Many attempts have been made, by the merchants of Bombay, to send this truly royal fruit to England. A case of mangoes was forwarded overland as a present to her Majesty, at Windsor, packed in cotton wool, and hermetically sealed, but whether they arrived sound or not, I never learned. Guavas, custard-apples, figs, and shaddocks are plentiful at this season, and pines, though not to be compared to our English fruit, are very common, and may be purchased for an anna or two. One great reason why the pine-apple here is coarse and indifferent in flavour is, the little attention bestowed upon its culture by native gardeners. The crown is simply cut off, and struck into the soil again, and Nature is allowed to nurse it in her own way, without any assistance from man. Plantains we have in Bombay, all the year round. They are very good fried, and are a wholesome and nutritious fruit. Oranges and grapes do not appear to grow well on the island, and Poonah supplies the tables of the rich at Bombay with these universal favourites.

Towards the close of the monsoons the rains are light and mild, and bright sunshine intervenes between the showers. In general, the rains are more abundant in the first, than in the second half of the season. They pour down at Bombay in torrents for many hours together, sometimes for days at their commencement; after which, about sunset, the weather clears up, and very little rain falls during the night. As the wet and dry season, in this part of India, is not regulated by the position of the sun, but by the change in the trade winds, a greater abundance of rain falls here, than in those countries which lie without the tropics and are subject to what are called variable rains. In this case, the season of the rains depends entirely on the position of the sun; beginning before the sun reaches the zenith of a place, and continuing for some time after it has passed it. We find from observation, that countries lying near the equator, are never for many days without rain, and that in those that are situated more than 5 deg. of latitude from the line, the seasons are generally distinctly marked.

From the rapid decomposition of vegetable matter, a sickly and trying season is now introduced at Bombay, and is much dreaded by Europeans residing at out-stations, or in the jungle. From the same cause, the atmosphere is filled with poisonous miasma, destructive to the health of the inhabitants; and agues and the jungle-fever spread amongst those that are exposed to the infected air. In the low districts, where the rains have been excessively heavy, many large tracts being flooded a foot or two deep, the exhalations load the atmosphere with a vapour so dense, as to obscure the stars at night. Dysentery, also, is now prevalent, more perhaps at this critical period than at any other; which may in a great measure be attributed to the abundance of green food. Soldiers are, on this account, forbidden to eat the fruit of the guava; that fruit being considered as very unwholesome, and as liable to produce this most distressing and dangerous disease. Great care is necessary, at this season, to guard against the sudden changes of temperature.

A great Hindoo festival is now celebrated, and known as cocoa-nut day. This holiday occurs on the 18th of August; at which time the season is supposed to open for traffic with the neighbouring coasts, and native boats may venture out to sea. It is a day of unusual excitement and merriment; and all Bombay is abroad to see the fair and the processions that take place. Thousands from all parts of the island, assemble upon the sea-shore in Back Bay, even so far as Malabar Point, being accompanied by priests, jogees, gosaens, and bearers and attendants, who bring with them gilt cocoa-nuts, flowers, mimic temples, deities, packages of cinnabar, and all sorts of things to be presented as offerings to the ocean. Faquirs; and a host of other idle and worthless characters, mad with opium, bhœng, and arrack, vary the amusements of the pleasure-seeking multitude, by acting the part of clowns in the most grotesque and ridiculous manner, with their faces, arms, and legs daubed with paint, and their bodies decked out with scraps of ragged finery. They make up a sort of procession, and go down to the sea, and cast in their gilt cocoa-nuts, which they try to make the unitiated in Hindoo mysteries and frauds believe, are of solid gold, but unfortunately they too often float. Temples, flowers, and tinsel ornaments, follow one another as propitiatory offerings; and every good Hindoo is now supposed to offer up a prayer to the effect, that when they venture once more to tempt the wave in their frail barks, success may attend their expeditions, and that they may never suffer shipwreck. After these vain ceremonies are over, the roads are once more lined with thousands who are making their way to the native village, where a grand fair and festival is going on in honour of the day. The night is usually passed in drunkenness and rioting by the rabble portion; though the respectable Hindoo, after prostrating himself in the temple, or bathing in the sacred tank, returns home at an early hour to recount the many events witnessed to the female portion of his family; women being seldom allowed to participate in those pleasures so eagerly sought after by their selfish lords. It is a curious sight to stroll along the shore the day after this festival of cocoa-nuts, and find it covered for miles with heaps of painted wood, flowers, and tinsel, which the ocean, one would fancy, had indignantly cast back again upon the beach; after this day a few of the fool-hardy venture out on their short fishing excursions, though the storms of the last three months still continue unabated. The monsoon is not over until the end of September; and no sensible merchant will allow his vessel to go to sea until after the Elephanta gales have passed away; yet the Hindoo sailors look now upon shipwreck as impossible, as they feel a sort of conviction, after this ceremony, that old Father Ocean's anger has been appeased, and if any of them are lost through their religious belief, which is often the case, particularly during the dreadful hurricanes of the Elephanta, it is put down to the score of not having made a proper offering.

And now, for many weeks the country is rich and lovely in all the glories of its floral productions, and India may, in very truth, be called a land of sunshine and flowers. Perhaps there are few countries where flowers are more loved and thought of. They enter into all Indian feasts and festivals! Turbans are ornamented with bunches of the large white jessamine, tied up with a rose in the centre; flowers are strewed over the marriage-bed, and hung in wreaths round the necks of the favourite deities in all the temples and sacred places.

I have now brought the monsoons to a close, and have endeavoured to recall a few events connected with this remarkable feature of the Indian year. From their termination to February, the cold months occur, but they are hardly to be distinguished from the hot and dry season that follows. The coast of Bombay experiences the full effects of the south-west monsoon. In July the rain increases in quantity, and may be said to attain its maximum. Slowly decreasing in August, and more rapidly in September, it departs amidst terrific thunder-storms about the first or second week in October.

CHAPTER IV.

"AND near those mighty temples stand,
The miracles of mortal hand,
Where hidden from the common eye
The past long buried secrets lie;
Those mysteries of the first great creed
Whose mystic fancies were the seed
Of every wild and vain belief
That held o'er man their empire brief."

The Old Temples of India. Hypogæa, or Subterraneous Caverns. Traditions of the East. Priests and People. Temples of Aboo. Why Islands were selected. Pious journeyings. Mr. and Mrs. H. Missionary-bit fanatics. A Pic-nic. Beauties of an Indian morning. Scenery in the harbour. Native boats. Sea Birds and picturesque objects. Closer view of Elephanta. The Landing. Delicious shade from the Sun. Stone Horse and Elephant. The handiwork of Father Time. Tamarind Tree and Flowers. Punkah Painting. Native Village. Excavated Rock. Birds of Night. Landscape changes. The Great Temple of Elephanta. Tale of a Tiger. Description of the Interior of the Cavern. Parting with Friends, &c., &c.

THE old temples of India have long claimed from the antiquary a large share of attention; not only on account of the peculiarity of their construction, but also because the period of their erection appears in almost every case to be involved in the deepest obscurity. The hypogæa, or subterraneous cavern structures, concerning which we have, at present, to speak, are, perhaps, the most remarkable monuments of human labour and perseverance to be met with in Asia. Their prodigious extent, massiveness of structure, and variety of design, lead us almost to doubt whether many of them were not originally natural cavities, enlarged and beautified by the hand of man. In the mountains of the Soubah of Cashmere, no fewer than twelve thousand of these grotto caverns have been explored, and found to be composed of a series of apartments and recesses supposed to be hewn out of the solid rock. Those of Kailasa, near Ellora, which are 247 feet long, and nearly 15 wide, are said to contain all the mythological deities of the Hindoos, though much injured and defaced by time. Many of them contain statues of colossal dimensions, and their walls are covered over with elaborate embellishments of the most fanciful description. But we can place no dependance on the current traditions of the East respecting them, and it would be fruitless to attempt to trace their early history. The ancient chronologers of India would seem to have had extraordinary notions of time; seeing that they tell us of kings, who reigned thousands of years; and of rajahs, who attained an age far beyond the nine hundred and sixty-nine years of the Methuselah, mentioned in the sacred Scriptures. The Brahmins are regarded by the people of India, as were the monks of old in our own country, as oracles of wisdom and piety. They alone are believed to have power to reveal the secrets of the past, or to draw aside the curtain which mercifully shrouds the future from human eyes. Their statements and writings only serve yet further to perplex the confused accounts that have been handed down from past ages, and to make our conjectures more uncertain and unsatisfactory. Thus, the wonderful mountain-caves and temples, situated near the once flourishing, but now nearly deserted city of Dowlatabad, are said to have been built by one Ecloo, Rajah of Ellichpore, and to be seven thousand nine hundred years old; such, at least, is the antiquity assigned to them by the venerable priests who generally conduct the visitor over these Hindoo temples—once, doubtless, thronged by worshippers—now, lonely and silent. The temples of Aboo, a lofty mountain range about forty miles from the military station of Deesa, in Guzerat, have not been long discovered, and are peculiarly interesting to the traveller from the circumstance of their all being carved out of black marble; but they have just as doubtful a date assigned to them as those of Dowlatabad, though, perhaps, (the hardness of the materials of which they consist being taken into account,) with more probability. It is necessary to bear in mind, that structures of this description suffer very little from exposure to the dry atmosphere of a country like India. In our own humid climate, the case is widely different. Here we sometimes find churches and public buildings crumbling into decay in the course of a single century; and even the vaunted stone of Caen, in Normandy, cannot withstand the "skiey influences" of two. It may appear, at first sight, singular, that a people so skilful in the fine arts as, if we may judge by these beautiful monuments of a past generation, must have been the inhabitants of Hindostan, should have selected such lonely and uncouth places for the site of their idol temples. Islands, subterranean caves, and almost inaccessible mountains, appear to have been their favourite localities for the erection of buildings, which, as we cannot doubt, were intended as places for the daily celebration of their peculiar worship. It is, however, to be considered, that, from time immemorial, India has been a prey to marauding chiefs and lawless usurpers, who robbed, desolated, or destroyed almost every important place, which they visited in their frequently occurring predatory excursions. Many of the idols set up in these temples during the hours of devotion were thought to be of great value; and it is not uncommon even now to see them formed of gold or silver, having for eyes diamonds and other precious stones. These idols offered great temptations to the plunderer; and it was necessary, therefore, in order to carry on the ceremonies inculcated in the sacred Vedas, and, at the same time, to preserve the riches of the temple from the spoiler's hand, that these buildings should be erected in places presenting great natural advantages in the way of security. The officiating priests and other officers connected with these religious establishments were accustomed to reside upon the spot, in rooms set apart for their accommodation; and the deluded worshippers who came, often laden with offerings, to pray, cared little for distance, or for the difficulties of the road; seeing that the more dangers they encountered in these their pious journeyings, the more acceptable they believed their service to be. Of the licentious character of the rites celebrated in these Pagan temples, it is needless here to speak. They have passed away. Enough, however, remains to show us their nature—while wandering over some of these ruinous structures, once polluted by the exercise of a vile and debasing superstition, and crowded by a degraded multitude—who were even, we may conclude, little better than the people of Sodom, and like unto those of Gomorrah, the words of the prophet Jeremiah flashed across my mind:—"Every man is brutish in his knowledge: every founder is confounded by the graven image: for his molten image is falsehood—they are vanity and the work of others: in the time of their visitation THEY SHALL PERISH."* Having said thus much in

* The Right Rev. M. Russell, in his views of ancient and modern Egypt, says—"There is a striking resemblance known to subsist between the usages, the superstitions, the arts, and the mythology of the ancient inhabitants of Western India, to those of the first settlers on the Upper Nile. The temples of Nubia, for example, exhibit the same features, whether as to style of architecture or the form of worship to which they were devoted, with the similar buildings which have been recently

reference to the ancient religious buildings scattered over India, I shall now proceed to describe a delightful excursion to the island of Gorapori, better known, perhaps, for reasons that will appear hereafter, by the familiar name of Elephanta.

It was about three months after the monsoons had ceased to deluge the land, that I received a note of invitation to spend an evening in the Fort, to meet a few friends, and particularly a Mr. and Mrs. H., who had just come down from Poonah. All the great people had gone to the Mahableshwur hills; the commander-in-chief having set the example by

examined in the neighbourhood of Bombay. In both cases they consist of vast excavations hewn out in the solid body of a hill or mountain, and are decorated with huge figures which indicate the same powers of nature, or serve as emblems to denote the same qualities in the ruling spirits of the universe. As a further proof of this hyphothesis, we are informed that the sepoys, who joined the British Army in Egypt, under Lord Hutchinson, imagined that they found their own temples in the ruin of Dendera, and were greatly exasperated at the natives for their neglect of the ancient deities whose images are still preserved. So strongly, indeed, were they impressed with this identity, that they proceeded to perform their devotions with all the ceremonies practised in their land. There is a resemblance, too, in the minor instruments of their superstition—the lotus, the lingam, and the serpent—which can hardly be regarded as accidental; but it is, no doubt, in the immense extent, the gigantic plan, the vast conception which appears in all their sacred buildings, that we most readily discover the influence of the same lofty genius, and the endeavour to accomplish the same mighty object. The excavated temples of Guerfeh Hassan, for instance, remind every traveller of the cave of Elephanta. The resemblance, indeed, is singularly striking; as are, in fact, all the leading principles of Egyptian architecture, and that of the Hindoos. • • • By whom and by what means these wonderful efforts have been accomplished, is a mystery sunk too deep in the abyss of time ever to be revealed," proceeding thither in great state, surrounded by a numerous retinue. Those who did not like the trouble of climbing these mountains, that rise to an elevation of some 5036 feet to the south of Bombay, or who perhaps could not afford to follow in the wake of the *Burro Saib*, but who were nevertheless anxious to avoid the inconveniences which, at Poonah, and in the neighbourhood, attend the hot season, generally stepped into their palanquins early in the morning; and, dismissing their bearers at the foot of the ghauts, proceeded by a fast coach to Panwelly and Bombay, the whole distance being only 75 or 80 miles. Some came to visit their children, who were placed at good boarding-schools, conducted by English masters; some for change of air, and sea-bathing; and others, to avoid being enrolled in the non-fashionable list of keepers-at-home; to stay quietly at home for a whole year being looked upon as a thing exceedingly *outré* by the military and merchant princes of the East; who, so great is the cost of travelling in *style* in India, annually expend enormous sums in pleasurable excursions. I must here introduce to my readers the two persons whom I have especially mentioned as being present on the occasion to which I have alluded—characters seldom met with in that gay country. Mr. and Mrs. H. had passed the greater part of their lives in India, and were singularly attached to the country in which they had acquired a competent share of wealth, with little injury to their originally Scottish constitutions. Being childless, and having no particular inducements to return to their native land, they had purchased or built a cool bungalow in the neighbourhood of Poonah, and lived not for themselves alone, but for the poor benighted heathen around them; devoting to their advantage, as I afterwards learned, certain days in every week, and a large portion of an honourably acquired fortune. These worthy people had resisted or avoided the temptations into which so many fall in the early part of their Indian career, and had passed unscathed through the fire. It were little to say of them that they were regular in their habits, strictly honourable in their engagements, and above the folly of attempting to outshine others, at the expense of living beyond their own means. They were, in fact, *Christians*, not only in name but in reality; and, as such, pursued the even tenor of their way, with one fixed purpose in view—the attainment of that rest which remaineth for the people of God.—They cared little for the scoffs and sneers of the world, by whom they were regarded as enthusiasts and *missionary-bit fanatics;* and were ever ready to return good for evil. The broken-down officer, who, in his days of prosperity, had *cut* them as not being persons of *ton*, found a shelter under their hospitable roof; and the gay and thoughtless cadet, who once had laughed at their wise saws and Scottish proverbs, lived to thank them for snatching him from early destruction, and to acknowledge them the instruments of his advancement to situations of honour and usefulness. In company, these excellent persons were extremely cheerful; retaining, however, a little of the stiffness and formality of the old English school of manners. The good lady's dress, too, exhibited the fashions of a bygone age; and her husband's conversation turned much upon occurrences scarcely remembered by the present generation. He spoke of railways, as of something, the consequences of which it was difficult to fathom; and feared, not altogether, perhaps, without reason, that in a few years they would quite change the character of his countrymen, and give them a dangerous taste for pleasuring, and spending their Sundays and holidays in the French metropolis. He remembered the arrival of the Marquis of Cornwallis in India, and had been at the first party given by Lord George Bentinck, when all the native gentry were first invited to meet the English officers, and were placed upon a proper footing in society, with the Londoners of Leadenhall Street.—During the very agreeable evening which I passed in the society of these excellent persons, it was proposed, that as there were several persons present who did not reside in Bombay, and who had seen little of the charming scenery in its neighbourhood, we should arrange a pic-nic party for the morrow; and the *Island of Elephanta* was at length fixed upon as the place to be visited. We separated, therefore, with the understanding, that we should meet at seven on the following morning, at the *Apollo Bunda*, where a fine boat, well secured from the sun, was to be engaged.

By gun-fire, the next day, I was up and ready.—

The morning was lovely; but this, by-the-bye, is an unnecessary and truly English observation, and one which I was heartily laughed at for making, on meeting a friend in India—*all* mornings being lovely there. On the present occasion, the gardens and compounds were refreshed by the heavy night-dews, and the fierce sun had not yet scorched the face of nature. The wild gourd still spread out its broad leaves over the natives' huts; and the grape-leafed castor-oil tree, laden with crimson clumps of spiny seed-vessels, appeared to be greener than ever; and the cloudless sky was reflected from its azure depth upon the bosom of a flowing tide, which came stealing onward, in gentle ripples, towards the shore. Groups of children were scampering about naked in the water, and allowing the waves to roll over them, as they swam out into the sea, and floated back again, to coax their swarthy little companions, who were splashing each other, to venture out further into the deliciously cool element. Through the opening in my tent, made to admit at pleasure the grateful breeze of the morning, I could command the view across Back Bay as far as Malabar-point, where, as I observed, a flag was floating in the grounds attached to the residence of the Governor of Bombay, who had given a sumptuous entertainment on the previous evening, and the returning carriages of whose guests had disturbed me during the night. Perched upon a piece of rock not yet covered by the advancing tide, a party of oyster-catchers were pluming their feathers, and spreading out their wings to dry; and dozens of sand-pipers and other aquatic birds were to be seen sporting near the low, bushy mangroves, and feasting upon the marine insects which infest their leaves.— The *pawney wallahs* were preparing for the daily supply of the different houses and tents, by filling their sheep-skin bags with water, at the large tanks on the esplanade; and a camel-driver was leading back to the encampment under the walls, a poor stray camel, that limped a good deal, as if foot-sore from a long journey over rough mountain-passes. Precisely as the hour of seven was tolled from the lofty tower of the English Cathedral in the Fort, I was upon the Apollo Bunda, and joined a few friends, who had been equally punctual with myself; nor had we long to wait for the rest of the party. It proved, however, as it always does, whenever a pic-nic party musters, that a great many necessary articles had been forgotten. First, it was discovered that Mr. C., the musical man of the party, had forgotten his cornopia. The case, indeed, had been duly sent down to the water-side, but the instrument was missing. Next, we found that we had no powder-flask among us, and that there were no percussion-caps to fit the pistols that were to be discharged in the caves; and lastly, it appeared that no gentleman had brought a cork-screw. To supply these various deficiencies took time: and it was nearly eight o'clock, before, satisfied that all the materials for the day's entertainment were on board, we pushed off from the pier, and paddled out into the bay, so as to obtain the full benefit of a flowing tide, and of the slight breeze which attended it. The heat, even at this comparatively early hour, was most oppressive, and the ladies' punkahs were put upon active service, as we slowly drifted past the walls of the Fort. Mr. and Mrs. H. had declined to take part in our excursion, but had promised to meet us in the evening, and learn the events of the day.

The scenery around us was striking; on our right was the Mahratta shore, with the high western chain of ghauts towering above it; on our left was Bombay with its spires, and mosques, massive fortifications, and old Mohammedan tombs, glittering in the bright morning sun; with here and there an enormous cocoa-nut tree rising majestically from the mass of public buildings; behind us was the open sea and Colabah; and before us a strange little mound or green hillock, peeping above the waters, and known to many as Cross or Gibbet Island; some notorious pirates having once paid there the penalty of their crimes; and not far off were Butcher's Island and *Elephanta*. My satisfaction was for a moment interrupted by our passing close under the stern of a large English ship, which had "Liverpool" painted under her counter. My beloved country, so many thousand miles distant, was at once forcibly recalled to my recollection; so easily will a trivial circumstance change the current of our thoughts, and cast a shadow on the brightest hours which we enjoy upon earth.

Anchored around us were some strange rigged

vessels from the Red Sea and Persian Gulf, Arabian built, with high prows; and each ornamented by a huge figure of some favourite idol, curiously carved. These vessels had brought over for sale, horses, and other products of their conntry; all which find a ready market in Bombay. Here were native boats, with mat-covered houses on deck, and laden with billets of wood from the Malabar coast, to supply the funeral pyres, which may be seen of an evening, in Back Bay, blazing high up into the heavens. From the sides of these vessels were hung several pumpkins, large enough to have accommodated, with ease, two or three Cinderellas. There were also nets of onions, cocoa-nuts, &c., from which might be inferred the nature of the sailors' fare while on board. A few fishing-boats kept us company for about two miles. The fishermen had caught some fine *pomfret* and *bumbalo* for the supply of the markets on the island. The rude and primitive character of their nets and tackle, the boats, and wild-looking dress of those on board, recalled to my remembrance the passage in St. Mark's Gospel, in which our Saviour is spoken of as walking on the Sea of Galilee, and seeing Simon and Andrew his brother casting a net into the sea; and then came the thought, that though eighteen centuries had rolled away since our blessed Saviour promised to make his disciples "fishers of men," the poor benighted men before me were utterly ignorant of those great and saving truths which were destined, in the fulness of time, to be spread, not only "throughout all the regions round about Gallilee," but throughout the whole of the habitable globe! Truly, "the harvest is indeed plenteous, but the labourers are few."

A species of sea-eagle and some other large birds were at this time wheeling over our heads, and occasionally diving down into the deep blue waves, as their keen eyes detected, among the small fry that sported there, any fitting prey; then they would shoot up again, with a "ha-ha," like the note of our laughing-gull, into the azure sky, and there remain poised, and motionless. It was the first time I had seen so much of the rich beauty of Indian scenery. In whatever direction the eye wandered, some charming and picturesque object presented itself, till the retina was almost pained by the quick succession of brilliant and glowing images. The rich tints of the distant mountains, clothed in their emerald herbage—the islands around us—the City of Bombay and its shipping in the distance—the sea—the heavens—all contributed to form a picture indescribably beautiful; I gazed—and gazed—and could scarcely help exclaiming—

> "These are thy glorious works, Parent of Good!
> Almighty! Thine this universal frame,
> Thus wondrous fair. Thyself how wondrous then!
> Unspeakable! who sitt'st above these heavens,
> To us invisible, or dimly seen, in
> These thy lowest works: yet these declare
> Thy goodness beyond thought, and power divine!"

On drawing near to Elephanta, I was enraptured

by a closer view of that island, fringed with palms to the water's edge, and having the sides of its lofty conical hills covered by a variety of plants, that were to me unknown. Patches of bare rock near the shore, relieved, however, by over-shadowing brushwood and luxuriant creepers, and here and there affording, by their many fissures, firm hold for a solitary cocoa-nut tree, gave a truly oriental character to the landscape. It was in vain that you tried to liken it to any English scenery; these trees effectually broke the spell. The boat was steered into a little bay or creek, where some of the inhabitants of the island had assembled to witness our debarkation, and had kindly waded in up to their arm-pits to pull the boat as high as possible on to the strand. Some children added a little to our amusement just at this place, by leaping into the sea from a piece of rock, and diving for a considerable way across the passage we were cautiously steering through. We had now been just two hours upon the water, and some of our party began to long for the cool wells of Elephanta's caves, and their embowering shades. A gentleman, who was an old resident in Bombay, and who had taken charge of many a merry party to this island, promised to introduce us to all its beauties, and to elucidate the many curious matters which we were about to see. Mr. C. was a member of that peculiar grade of Indian Society, who have sprung from European fathers by native mothers. He had been well educated, was an accomplished and agreeable man, and had delighted us during the voyage with scraps of a most romantic and singular life. He was, in fact, one of those nondescript personages so often met with in our Eastern presidencies, who know everything, and are known by everybody.

After some little difficulty we effected a landing on the eastern side of the island; which landing, however, was rendered rather dangerous and disagreeable from the circumstance that the spring tide partly covered numbers of huge rocks and stones which had, in the course of time, been severed from the mountain, and which had rolled down below high-water-mark. To keep the boat clear of these impediments, and run her as near as possible to the shore, had been a work of much anxiety to the owners; for Indian pleasure-boats of this description are but slightly built, and will not stand much grinding on a gravelly bottom. As it was, we gentlemen had to wade on shore; so that the boat, thus lightened, might float to a little jetty of rocks which enclosed a fishing ground, and upon which the ladies were enabled to land. Once more upon terra firma, we gave into the charge of two servants who had accompanied us, the baskets of eatables; and having selected, out of ten or a dozen people eager for the office, one guide who professed to talk a little English, but who generally lapsed into bad Mahratta before he had finished a sentence, we proceeded in single file up a narrow foot-path, half hid by low prickly shrubs and trees, and affording a delicious shade after the half-hour's exposure upon the sunny beach. Had we landed on the other side of the island, we should have been spared the trouble of going round to see the celebrated stone *elephant*, which is carved out of the solid rock, and which has given an imperishable name to this island. This figure has been split into parts; but whether by accident or design, appears to be very doubtful. Some attribute this act to the Portuguese; since they, on their invasion of India, are believed to have considered it a religious duty to destroy every object connected with the pagan worship of the natives. The statue of the Elephant is situated on the acclivity of a hill, about 250 yards from the water, and no doubt was the first object of worship to those landing on the island. Among the Hindoo deities we find that Ganesa, who is a portly personage with the head of an elephant, was at one time so honoured and revered, that no religious work could be undertaken without first invoking a blessing from him. Hence we may conclude, that the stone elephant here had peculiar honours paid to him before the devotees climbed the hill to the temple. Time is fast completing the destruction of this interesting relic of a past age. In 1814, the head and neck became disunited from the colossal trunk; and this portion of the figure lies partly buried in the sandy soil. Some attribute this second misfortune to a slight shock of an earthquake; others to the gradual decay of the black stone out of which the statue is carved; and this last opinion appears to be reasonable; for, with a little effort, it is easy to detach large scales from the stone. But writers on the antiquities of this island think, that the splitting of the figure was caused by gunpowder, and was the work of the Portuguese in their religious zeal to annihilate every memorial here. Not far from the elephant stands the figure of a horse cut out from the same material, and called the "Horse of Alexander;" in memory, as some suppose, of Alexander the Great, to whom, with no greater probability, as Mr. Dalrymple observes, have also been attributed the excavations to which this island owes its celebrity. Alexander, as I should imagine, in the midst of his great designs and great achievements, had matters of more importance to attend to, than the carving of Hindoo deities in this unimportant island. Be this as it may, the stone horse of Elephanta is still attributed to him; and as India, and perhaps this part of it, was one of his last conquests, it is just possible, that this hero of a thousand battles might pay a visit to this small island, and record the event upon one of its rocky hill-sides after the fashion of the Romans.

But to proceed; we found the path very steep and rugged, and moreover encumbered by loose stones; the late rains having, as our guide informed us, carried away much of the soil, and thus rendering our footing very insecure. We saw some very fine tamarind trees, hung with their thin long green pods, but not sufficiently ripe to be gathered. The tamarind is a beautiful spreading tree; its leaves are wing-shaped or pinnated abruptly, being composed of sixteen or eighteen pairs of green leaflets growing on the stem, and covered with a fine silky down. Its flowers grow in loose bunches, and rise from the sides of the branches; the calix and petals are of a yellow tinge, variegated with red veins; the fruit, which is rather a valuable article of export, is generally preserved in India without any syrup. The natives entertain some strange ideas respecting this tree, and tell you that it is very dangerous to sleep under it during the night. Many splendid flowers here attracted my attention; some had fine trumpet-shaped blossoms, wide enough to cover a breakfast cup. That curious palm, the *Chamærops humilis*, or *Corypha umbracula* of botanists, better known as the punkah, or fan-palm, spread out its circle of united leaves, proceeding from a short, stiff foot-stalk. This plant appeared to flourish well here; for we saw dozens of it in various stages of growth; some so young as not to have burst from their cases; others, many feet high, and stiff and dry to the touch; sounding like card-board when struck. There was something so very artificial about these vegetable wonders, fringed round with a sort of defensive armour like spear points, that it was difficult to believe they were actually growing. The Hindoos have converted them to many useful purposes; the large plants are used for roofing, and the small are dried in the sun for hand-punkahs, shades, &c. The Chinese gather them very young, and place them in a press, where they remain till quite dry, and sufficiently flat to be painted upon. Birds and figures are often beautifully executed upon them; after which they are highly varnished, shaped into fans or screens, and attached to ornamented handles. The inferior leaves have the natural stalk for a handle, and can be purchased for an *anna*, or so, in the bazaars at Bombay. In situations favourable to its growth and free expansion, this palm attains a considerable size, and adds much to the beauty of Indian forest-scenery, casting a grateful shadow over the weary wayfarer when the sun has risen upon the earth.

After a quarter of an hour's journey up the steep path-way that wound between two hills rising abruptly on both sides of us, which journey was diversified by many falls, and by other disasters, of such a kind, however, as rather to increase the merriment of our party, we suddenly came within view of a village composed of a rambling collection of mud huts, not unlike those seen in the North of Ireland, and, to all appearances, as *neat* and *comfortable*. Some wretched-looking women came out to take a peep at us, attended by thirty or forty jackall-bred dogs, who set up a howl loud enough to be heard all over the island. As these dogs came dashing through the jungle towards us, I raised my gun and took a steady aim at the most daring; but no sooner did he suspect my intention, than he turned tail, followed by the pack, and away they set off full gallop down the hill, and were soon lost to observation amidst the tangled foliage below us. The inhabitants of this lone village, the only one I believe on the island, appeared to be a race quite different from those of Bombay; and as we saw many fishing nets spread out to dry, I concluded, that they derived their principal support from the sea that surrounds them. Having walked about a quarter of a mile further, we halted under the shadow of an overhanging rock, in which was excavated a large chamber. On each side of the entrance to this chamber, were rude figures which had once represented men, but which were now defaced, and almost destroyed by long exposure to the atmosphere; besides being overgrown by the roots and branches of trees that shot out from the rock above them. The doorway formed an imperfect triangle, (a figure seen in Egyptian architecture) but without the projecting slab on the top. I peeped in, but was repelled, by its very uninviting appearance, from exploring this chamber, the floor and sides of which were coated with a slimy sort of mud that had filtered through the hill; besides this, some one spoke of snakes and centipedes as taking up their lodging there; and that decided me at once. There seemed to be a rude altar erected in the centre; but all was gloomy, and of course very indistinctly seen from the outside. I threw in a few stones, which had the effect of startling two or three strange birds, which flew out, and disappeared quickly in the woods, as if not accustomed to the glare of broad day.

We rested here some time, the view from this elevated position being very imposing and extensive. Dark shadows were cast upon the sea from the adjoining land; and the objects on the Mahratta coast, which before had been but indistinctly seen, were now brought out into fine relief by the sunshine, which quite changed the character of the landscape, though without in the least detracting from its beauty. There was a sweet tranquillity about the place at this hour. Everything that had life had sought the shade of the woods; and even the gaudy butterfly, that "child of the sun," had folded his burnished and many-tinted wings, and had hid himself, for protection, in the cups of the drooping flowers; the very air was still, and laden with grateful odours. As it was noon, the heat was intense, and some of our party were but little inclined to leave the shade of the rock, which, with its overhanging foliage, formed a gorgeous canopy above us. A brief walk, however, brought us into a fresh path, which wound round the mountain, and led us to its opposite side. Here the scenery bore a different character; and the gentlemen of the party had to walk first, in order to beat down, with sticks, the long arrow-grass and prickly thorns, before it was possible for the ladies to attempt to descend the hill. However, with some slight difficulties, such as the tearing of veils, and catching of flounces, we made our way through these obstacles that concealed the pathway and the guide, and found ourselves suddenly standing before the great cavern pagoda, or

Temple of Elephanta—a place which once boasted of more pilgrims to its many shrines, than ever visited the shrine of the holy prophet at Mecca. We were all glad that our fatigues were over, and no one, perhaps, more so than myself; for I had not yet become inured to the climate. Heated as we were, we all felt afraid of exposing ourselves too soon to the cool temperature of the inviting cavern that yawned before us; so while we sat resting ourselves, one of our party beguiled the time by relating an anecdote having reference to the Island of Salsette, of which, from the elevated spot which we occupied, we had an excellent view. This anecdote, as it has strict truth to recommend it, I shall now present to my readers; and we may call it a

TALE OF A TIGER.

Some years ago (for I cannot be certain as to the exact time), a party of officers from the barracks were strolling along shore, near Sion Fort, Bombay, when one of them, who was on the look-out for stray game, perceived *something*, which had evidently left Salsette, swimming towards Bombay; and, to all appearance, likely to land near the spot on which they stood. As the natives never bathe in this bay, on account of the sharks which infest it, the whole party felt satisfied that *it was not a man*. On a sudden, it altered its course, and landed higher up than was expected; when, greatly to the astonishment of the officers, they saw that it was neither more nor less than a fine, full-grown tiger. The beast, having given himself two or three shakes, like a Newfoundland dog, trotted quietly up the beach, towards some small cottages, and seized, near the door of one of them, a little child who was there playing, and whom he had no doubt marked as he was swimming. The shrieks of the terrified child brought out from the cottages a few persons, who, however, on learning the circumstances of the case, disappeared again as quickly as they had come. The officers, two or three of whom had fire-arms, boldly hastened towards the scene of danger; but before they had got within shot of him, the monarch of the jungle quitted his hold of the child, walked back quietly to the sea, and had swam about twenty yards back again, when a ball from a rifle put a stop to his progress. He reared up in the water, plunged violently once or twice, and then disappeared beneath the discoloured waves. A canoe was soon procured; and after some trouble the noble animal was dragged on shore in triumph, amid the cheers of numbers who had been attracted to the spot. The skin was taken to Bombay, and the officer who had shot the tiger received a good sum from the East India Company. The sum they had offered for every lion and tiger shot in the country, was, I believe, twenty pounds for a lion, and fifteen for a tiger; but I am not quite certain as to the amount. This was the last tiger killed or seen near Bombay, and was supposed to have swum over to Salsette from the main land; as that island, after this invasion, was pretty well hunted up, by many an adventurous party, in the hope of gaining a similar reward, but without success. This little story was related to me by a brother of the gallant officer of the rifle. The child, most fortunately, was more frightened than hurt.

During the time occupied by the relation of this thoroughly Indian anecdote, and by the conversation to which it gave rise, our party had become cool; and, accordingly, we prepared to enter

THE CAVE.

Numberless pilgrimages have been made by the lovers of antiquities, to this subterranean temple, termed by Mr. Maurice, "the wonder of Asia," the excavation of which has been attributed to Semiramis, as well as to the great Alexander. Three spacious entrances are afforded between four rows of massive columns in the brow of the hill, about half-way up its steep ascent from the shore. For a few seconds after entering the cave, I could distinguish nothing; the change was so sudden, from the broad light outside, to the darkness within: but at length its extent and extraordinary sculptures gradually revealed themselves to my astonished gaze. I am anxious to present to my readers a minute and correct description of what I saw here, and I had each figure and compartment particularly explained to me at the time, by a gentleman well versed in the mythological history of Hindostan, yet as memory cannot be depended upon, and as my notes are imperfect with regard to the dimensions of the figures, and other matters of importance, I am indebted in this matter to Maurice, Niebuhr, and some other celebrated writers on India, for the following account of the interior:—"The length of this temple, measuring from the entrance, which is on the north-side, is 130 feet, and its breadth 123 feet: the floor not being level, the height varies from 15 to 17½ feet. The roof was supported by twenty-six pillars and eight pilasters, disposed in four rows; but several of the pillars are broken. Each column stands upon a square pedestal, and is fluted; but, instead of being cylindrical, is gradually enlarged towards the middle. Above the tops of the column a kind of ridge has been cut to resemble a beam about twelve inches square, and this is richly carved. Along the sides of the temple are cut between forty and fifty colossal figures, in height from twelve to fifteen feet—none of them being entirely detached from the wall. Some of those figures have on their head a kind of helmet; others wear crowns, with rich devices; and others again are without any other covering than curled and flowing hair. Some of them have four, and others six hands, holding sceptres, shields, symbols of justice, ensigns of religion, weapons of war, and trophies of peace. On the south-side, facing the entrance, is an enormous bust with three faces, representing the triple deity, Brahma, Vishneu, and Siva;—Brahma, the creator, occupies the centre position. This face measures five feet in length; the width from the ear to the middle of the nose is three feet four inches; the width of the whole figure is near twenty feet. On the right is the Preserver, Vishneu; and Siva, the destroyer, is on the left, having in his hand a Cobra Capella, or hooded snake, and on his cap a human skull. To the left of this bust, amid a group of uncouth figures, is one, a female form, to which Niebuhr has given the name of Amazon, from the fact of its being without the right breast. This figure has four arms. The right fore-arm rests upon the head of a bull; the left fore-arm hangs down, and once contained something which is now mutilated and undistinguishable. The hand of the right arm grasps a Cobra Capella, and that of the hinder left arm holds a shield." At the east end is a passage, about eighteen feet long, terminating in an open space that admits the light through a sort of shaft-hole in the rock, and containing a delicious spring of the finest water to be found in this part of India. As Bombay has long been proverbial for the badness of its water, the table of the governor is occasionally supplied from this delicious spring; and many who are about to sail from the country lay in a few dozens of it for the voyage, as it keeps well. The approach to this place is guarded by four figures, fourteen feet high; beautifully executed, and more perfect than any to be found in this temple. At the west end, and almost opposite the passage that leads to the well, is a room or recess about twenty feet square, having, in the centre of it, an altar, upon which are placed symbols of a worship, "offensive to European notions of delicacy." "The entrance to this recess is also guarded by eight naked figures, each 13½ feet high, sculptured in a manner which shows that the people by whom they were executed must have made considerable progress in the statuary's art." The whole of this portion of the excavation is in a very ruinous condition, and the roof appears to be fast sinking in; thus threatening a speedy destruction to this altar and its detestable accompaniments. The floor is heaped up with rubbish that has crumbled from the side walls; and has doubtless considerably diminished the height of the apartment. The same may be said of the other rooms. This, as my friend privately told me, is called the chamber of abominations. He also observed, that, even in his memory, the whole of the temple was much changed for the worse. The rains are permitted to lodge within them four months out of the twelve; though a day or two's labour, and a few rupees expended in making a proper drain, would secure these interesting monuments from destruction. He thought that when the pillars should give way, the mountain above must bury all. I heard it stated in Bombay, that when the Portuguese visited this island, they were so horrified by the character of this heathen temple, that they ordered a piece of heavily loaded cannon to be planted opposite the entrance, with the hope of destroying the principal pillars that support the roof, and burying the cave in the ruins of the mountain above it.

No such violence, however, is now needed. Like all the works of man, this wonderful excavation is fast crumbling away beneath the great Spoiler's hand. The rock itself is soft and powdery to the touch, and is fast perishing from age and long exposure to the atmosphere; and the cave has long been deserted by the infatuated worshippers of the strange gods which it contains; while the enormous sums said to be exacted by the priests and others connected with it, have, doubtless, been diverted into other channels. The triple figure has been to some writers a source of strange conjecture as to its real meaning, and was long supposed to represent the Hindoo triad; though many believe it to be simply a figure of Siva, to whom this temple, and almost all similar structures in the West of India, are dedicated. This temple is filled with the images and transformations of Siva, the god of destruction; and as we are now in the midst of the heathen gods and goddesses, a few words about the celebrated Hindoo trinity may not prove uninteresting to my readers. The sacred books of India distinctly recognise the existence of one supreme and invisible Author and Ruler of the universe; and Sir William Jones has furnished us with a translation of the Vedas, from some of whose texts we are enabled to glean their doctrines respecting the nature and attributes of the Deity. The following, extracted from the Gayatri, or holy passages, shows us what sublime ideas they entertained respecting the Great Invisible One.

"Let us adore the supremacy of that divine sun the Godhead, who illuminates all, who creates all, from whom all proceed, to whom all must return, whom we invoke to direct our understandings aright in our progress towards his holy seat.

"What the sun and light are to this visible world, that are the Supreme Good and Truth to the intellectual and invisible universe; and as our corporeal eyes have a distinct perception of objects enlightened by the sun, thus our souls acquire certain knowledge by meditating on the light of truth which emanates from the Being of Beings; that is the light by which alone our minds can be directed in the path to beatitude.

"Without hand or foot he runs rapidly, and grasps firmly; without eyes he sees; without ears he hears all; he knows whatever can be known; but there is none who knows him. Him the wise call the Great Supreme Pervading Spirit."

In the Hindoo trinity, Brahma, who stands at the head, is looked upon as the author of the world. He is represented as having produced everything out of himself, and all that was, or is, partakes of his essence. We cannot but smile at the history of his origin.—The Supreme mind is said to have deposited an egg in the waters, which it created, and which egg remained there inactive for many million years, till Brahma, who was snug inside of it, willed that its shell should break; and thus was he born in the form of a divine male, to be for ever famed, throughout all worlds, as the great forefather of spirits. Brahma, considering his high position, and his relation to the Supreme Mind, has but few honours paid him; only two or three temples having been erected to his especial service in India.

Vishnu, on the contrary, has many followers. He is represented in the sacred books as the Deliverer, ever ready to interpose between man and any danger that threatens his race. He is thought to descend frequently to this earth, in various animated forms: for marvellous and amusing are the transformations ascribed to him. He first made his appearance as a fish, of such small dimensions as to be easily placed in a chattee of water; but he gradually expanded, until a cistern, a pool, and a lake, were too small to hold this growing god. He was consequently thrown into the sea, where he destroyed a giant, and appeared blazing like molten gold, a million of leagues in extent. Changing here to a boar, he raised, with his tusks, from the bottom of the sea, our earth, and then sunk out of sight. Wonderful are the works ascribed to Vishnu; but we have quoted sufficient to satisfy the reader of their absurdity, and will now turn to the third member of the Hindoo triad, to whom the temple of Elephanta is supposed to be dedicated.

Siva is represented as of a bright silver colour—

sometimes having five faces, and at other times only one with three eyes. The history of his exploits are strange and unnatural; and a female partner is mixed up with his adventures, called Doorga, who is the principal of the female deities—a warlike and terrific creature, and originally called Parvati, until she slew the giant of that name who had made slaves of the gods, and destroyed him by causing nine millions of warriors to issue from her body, to fight against his army of a hundred millions of chariots, and one hundred and twenty millions of elephants. After this fierce contest, Parvati took the name of this huge enemy, which name was graciously bestowed on her by the emancipated gods.

Doorga and Kalee have more worshippers than any other god or goddess in India, and their temples flow with the blood of animal sacrifices. Decoits, thieves, and all the worst characters that spread terror throughout Hindostan, pay peculiar honours to this horrid woman, and her friend Kalee. They recognise the latter as the only goddess endued with power sufficient to protect them from discovery during their pillaging excursions. Consequently, Kalee is a most popular divinity, invoked by dark incantations for blessings and aid on every unlawful occasion or adventure in which Hindoo robbers engage. Elliot, speaking of the extraordinary superstitions of India, says, "If they did not create, they at least furnished the materials of the Grecian mythology, though softened and beautified by that poetical imagination, which formed, in ancient times, the golden age of poetry upon earth." The lines of Mrs. Maclean on this subject are doubtless familiar to many of my readers. In allusion to Eleora, and to the gloomy superstitions of the East, as well as to the aptitude of the Greeks,

"To turn, beneath their softer sky,
All that was faith to poetry;"

She thus writes:

"Hence had the Grecian fables birth,
And wandered beautiful o'er earth;
Till every wood, and stream, and cave,
Shelter to some bright vision gave;
For all of terrible and strange,
That from these gloomy caverns sprung,
From Greece receiv'd a graceful change,
That spoke another sky and tongue,
A finer eye, a gentler hand,
Than in their native Hindoo land."

Thousands of devotees are said to have paid annual visits to this temple of Elephanta, from all parts of the country; and even after the breaking up of its shrines, and the scattering of its priests, the cave was not entirely deserted by the deluded worshippers, who still fancied its headless gods had power enough left to hear their prayers, and to accept their vain oblations. Now, its glory has departed from it, and "the sound of the church-going-bell," stealing across the slumbering waters, from Bombay, is alone heard to echo among the mountains and caves, and once polluted temples, that formerly resounded to the fanatical howlings of its pilgrims, and the dinning *tom-tom* that attends their ceremonies. Death and time have here hushed all into silence. The people whose boast these wondrous structures must once have been, have long passed away, and their memory has long been forgotten in the land. Let us hope, that a brighter and happier day has dawned upon India, and that its poor and benighted people, so long neglected, may yet live to bless the means that are now working together for their good, and to worship the true and only God, who dwelleth not in temples made with hands.

We will now return to our party, whom we left unpacking baskets, and spreading out on a China mat the various matters we had brought from Bombay. Some of the ladies insisted on having coffee; and a *Kitmutgar* was accordingly sent to collect sticks, to make a fire to boil it; at which commission I remember he grumbled excessively, as it did not come within his regular code of duties as a head-table servant to perform such menial offices; however, by a little persuasion, and by the promise of some luxury, the name of which was unknown to me, he was induced to go, and soon returned with an armful of sticks, and an old soldier, who made us a profound salaam, and politely informed us in Hindostanee, that he was appointed governor of the island, and had charge of the caves, and that it was his duty to see that no one wantonly injured any of the figures. He was invited to partake of what he saw before him; and as soon as we had sufficiently refreshed ourselves, he requested us all to bend our steps towards the *Trimurti*, and hear the wonderful things he had to say concerning it. These things said; and they amounted to nothing more than what I have stated; he made us another very respectful salaam, and several to the individuals who, after the fashion of the gipsy, crossed his open palm with a shining rupee or two, and vanished as unexpectedly as he had appeared; leaving those who understood his language better than I did, exceedingly amused by his parting address. The heat had not destroyed our appetite, nor did the monster figures in the least scare us during the interesting service of dinner and tea combined. Humourous anecdotes related by the Anglo-Indian gave a zest to the entertainment, and songs and music now enlivened our little party. Some of these songs having reference to the country, I shall endeavour to present a free version of one of them, with all its imperfections, to my indulgent readers :—

Now panting nature seeks repose,
The sun sinks low, the night-flower blows
And scents the sultry air;
The camel near yon cotton tree,
Folds under him the wearied knee,
No burthen now to bear.

The vampire sails round temples old
Where legendary tale is told
Of Doorgas' fierce allies;
The bulbul sings his farewell song
From flowery shrub, whence all day long,
His grateful notes arise.

O'er woods and vallies with delight
The fire-fly bears his wandering light,
Now is his happy hour;
When flowers are left alone for him
To sip their sweets upon the wing
Within each dewy bower.

The buff'loe bellows on the plain,
And makes the forests shake again
As he walks forth and feeds;
For all day long within some pool
He laid his panting sides to cool
Amidst the jointed reeds.

Now prowling jackalls steal abroad;
The tiger and the lion lord
Lurk in the jungles near;
The peacock, brighten'd by yon ray
That decks the heavens at closing day,
Hides his plumed head in fear.

On nullahs' cypress-shaded brink,
The feverish herd come down to drink,
And bathe in waters pure;
The hunting Cheta creeps unseen,
And marks a victim in the stream;
His evening meal is sure.

But hark! what sound is that we hear
So softly falling on the ear?
It is an evening bell,
That swings in yonder mosque's old tower
Rising above the high palm bower,
For day now bids farewell.

The Hindoo to his prayers must go,
The lamps are lit in rows below,
And round about his god;
See now they kneel and make salaam,
Beside their Brahmin, holy man,
And kiss the place he trod.

All prostrate fall and mutter fast
Each prayer as if it were the last
That they should ever say;
While incense burns in niches round,
And flowers are strew'd upon the ground—
'Tis thus the Hindoos pray.

Man's labouring hours by shadows known
Upon the wings of time have flown:
He hies him to his cot;
Peace and tranquillity are there;
Regardless of the morrow's care,
Contentment is his lot.

The caves of Elephanta are, as it may be supposed, often visited; the island being only seven miles from Bombay Castle, and five from the Mahratta shore.—The English traveller is apt, it is said, to indulge, even here, his strange propensity to possess himself of relics, and is occasionally known to break off a nose or a finger, to carry home with him as a substantial proof of his having really visited this "wonder of Asia," and tiffened under the sacred rock of Gorapori.

The shadows of evening had stolen imperceptibly around us, before we broke up our party; and the rich notes of the cornopia breathed a sweet farewell to cave and hill. As we wended our way along the mountain-path towards the shore, I felt something like regret from the thought, that, in all probability, I should never again visit this beautiful island of the sea; and as we rowed slowly over the star-lit waters towards Bombay, there was something, at this witching hour, so calm and tranquil in the scene around us, that conversation soon ceased altogether; and each one among us seemed occupied by his own musings. We found our friends in the Fort anxiously awaiting our return; and after an hour or two spent very agreeably, I bade adieu to many who had contributed much to my happiness, both on this memorable day, and on former occasions. A sorrowful feeling oppressed me; for I had a painful conviction that some of us would never meet again in this world—a foreboding which has been realized; but

> "There are tones that will haunt us, though lonely
> Our path be, o'er mountain and sea;
> There are looks that will part from us only,
> When memory ceases to be."

CHAPTER V.

Farewell to the Monsoons. Silk cotton tree. Palms, Decanna bean. Orderiferous Pandanus, Orchids. Anxiety of the agriculturist. Irrigation. Dry and wet crops of the year. Early risers in Bombay. Muggy days. Heavy dews of night. Drooping of Leaves and Flowers. Insects. Tree Lizard, its habits. Bungalow Lizard. Large Kites. Snakes, Cobra Manilla. Death of an officer from bite of carpet snake. Scorpions. Spiders. Child killed. Centipedes. Hornets and wasps. Natural scavengers, their Visits to your cooking-house. Portuguese traps. Fine sense of smell in Fulvous Vulture. The Woods at noon. Brilliant plumage of birds. Loss of song. Alcedo Asiatica. Emerald Fly-catchers. Green Woodpeckers. Butcher birds, Hoopoe, Sandpiper. Wanton destruction of Indian birds, &c., &c.

THE rainy season has passed away; and the fearful storms that lately swept over the dark waters of the Indian Ocean, and hurled its billows with such terrific force upon the coast, have gradually subsided into a peaceful calm.

> " Mercy's voice has hushed the blast,"

and the low murmuring of the morning or evening breeze is alone heard amidst those forests, which, but a short time ago, bowed their sturdy limbs and pathless jungles to the raging of the monsoon. The scared jackal that fled before this dreaded enemy, the only invader of his profound solitude, returns again to his ancient haunts, and "seeks his food from God."—The luxuriant vegetation, which so suddenly clothed the surface of earth, painting the landscape with myriads of glorious blossoms of every hue, and which sprang suddenly into life during that remarkable period, is now fast drooping and dying around us; and the large crimson flowers of the lofty cotton-tree* have vanished, and given place to the bursting capsule with its silky treasure. Innumerable wild annuals have gone through the many stages of their short existence, and now wait the returning rains, to bid them once more spring forth, welcome to man as the voice of the turtle heard in the land. But in this fair country, where summer and winter can scarcely be distinguished from each other, and where the leaves of many trees are only shed to give place to new ones, the fading of the ephemeral visitors which perfect an Eastern landscape, are not regretted, as are, among ourselves, the productions of an English summer, when autumn shows her "sere and yellow leaf." The gorgeous palms, which Linnæus has justly entitled "the princes of the vegetable world," still rear their crowned pillars above us; and the peepul, palmyra, and the banyan cast their grateful shadows over the scorching glades; nor have flowers forsaken us. In moist districts in the interior, the Decanna-bean (*Butea Superba*) lights up with its glowing scarlet

* Bombax Ceiba.

blossoms the dark forests, and the odoriferous *Pandanus* scents the morning breeze. The glittering orchids, like butterflies sporting in air, and the magnificent dendrobiums, give a charm to Eastern scenery, and delight the eye by the richness and beauty of their colours. The decaying monarch of the jungle, rearing his blighted form amidst the profusion of humbler shrubs, is not here an object fit only for melancholy contemplation. The past storms have wafted the seeds of various graceful parasitical plants, and every rent or cranny in its aged trunk displays some curiously-tinted blossoms, which scent from their floating tendrils the moist atmosphere of the cool woods. Flourishing, as it were, upon the wreck of nature, these epiphytes seize upon the withering branches so favourable to their growth, and again clothe them in new and delicious apparel. A lovely species of *Trichozanthes* hangs its vivid scarlet fruit from the topmost branches of the forest, but this climbing plant only expands its white and fringed flower during the silent hours of night. The anxious agriculturist, who cast a wistful eye over the arid plains, which, in case the expected rains should be abundant, were to supply many thousands with food, and who, with a desponding sigh, saw the skins half filled with water from the failing reservoirs, emptied into the little channels that conducted the precious fluid to the planted fields of promise, again has had his wants supplied; and again the valleys stand so thick with corn, that they laugh and sing. The rice grounds which were prepared in March and April, ready to receive the seed in May, have long been reaped; and the exhausted corn-jars have again been replenished to satisfy the wants of those multitudes, who, while they live upon His gifts, refuse to give to God the glory.

It is necessary to bear in mind, that in a climate like that of India, a constant succession of the most beautiful crops might be produced, if, for the purposes of irrigation, a sufficient and regular supply of water could be ensured. Two seed-crops are, however, generally secured in the year. The first is the natural result of the periodical rains, and is called, the *khureef*, or wet crop, which is sown with the rice in May and June, and reaped about the end of October; and the second, assisted by artificial means, and called the *rubbee*, or dry crop, sown about the first week in November, and reaped in March and April. Rice, cotton, indigo, and maize, are sown before the monsoons commence; and wheat, barley, oats, millet, and other crops of smaller seeds, reward the labourer at all seasons of the year. Thus, the stranger is often astonished to see sowing and reaping going on at the same time, in fields not far apart from one another; yet with all this seeming plenty, famine, in its most dreadful shapes, has frequently stalked through this double-harvest-bearing land. The rice, upon which a third part of the vast population is fed, has perished for want of water, or has been devoured by the locusts; and the cattle and the labourer have expired together. Among the many desolating famines in India, of which history has furnished us with accounts, that which occurred in Bengal, in 1770, is the most harassing to contemplate; several millions of human beings being said to have perished in it. Another famine, that thinned the north-west provinces, proved almost as fatal; and had not the hand of charity, in a great measure, averted the calamity, by relieving daily 80,000 individuals at Agra, it would have been impossible to have calculated the amount of deaths. Such disastrous occurrences are, however, rarer now than they were formerly—the Indian husbandman having been taught the necessity of providing against the future, by storing up his corn in the seasons of plenty.* The rains are always variable and uncertain; some districts in the interior being flooded, while others are barely visited by passing showers. In Bombay, rain to the depth of thirty-two inches has been known to fall, during the first twelve days of the south-west monsoon; this being the average fall of a whole year in England. The consequence is, on such occasions, that every road and field is flooded, and that the new

* Corn in Guzerat is often stored up near the farmer's house, in large earthen jars, capable of holding the contents of three or four of our ordinary sacks. These jars are secured by a close-fitting lid, fastened down with clay or chunam, to prevent the ingress of the destructive white ants. Those which I first saw were arranged side by side under a shed, close by the owner's residence, and puzzled me much, before I could find out their use. The Arabian story of Ali-Baba, or the forty thieves, occurred to me, for each jar might easily have contained one, if not two, tall robbers.

town, from its low swampy situation, suffers severely. The reader will perceive that I have not confined my description entirely to the Island of Bombay. Agricultural farming is carried on on a very small scale here, the land being poor, and naturally producing little, excepting cocoa-nut trees, and some trifling articles of fruit. The inhabitants are chiefly supplied with vegetables, poultry, sheep, &c., from Salsette; and the teeming plains of Guzerat furnish them with corn, which is conveyed by sea, as all land carriage is very expensive and slow, on account of the wretched roads, and miserable mode of conveyance adopted in India. The cool and agreeable north-east monsoon that succeeds that of the south-west, or rainy wind, continues to blow steadily to the end of February.— Dry and fair weather is now certain throughout this great peninsula, though the north-east monsoon brings with it rain on the eastern side of the Coromandel coast, from October to December. To March the north-east winds prevail, in which month they gradually cease altogether, and irregular veering winds, attended by hot blasts and excessive and relaxing days, may be expected until the commencement of May or June. We will now return to our recollections of this hot season in Bombay, and of matters therewith connected.

The scene has changed: the sun so long obscured during the rainy months, or only peeping out between the dark masses of electric clouds, now bursts forth with redoubled power; and man begins to devise plans to meet the coming hot season, and to shade his dwelling as much as possible from its scorching rays. 'Tis early morn—day has just broken over the high eastern ghauts, and the welcome streak of light spreads rapidly over the lofty canopy above us. You have taken your bath, and feel a longing desire to go forth into the open air, to ramble through the compound, or, in fact, to escape, in whatever direction, from your confined bungalow, the walls of which have scarcely thrown off the heat of the past day. If early abroad, it is no uncommon thing to find everything enveloped in a hot steaming vapour, that strongly recalls to the memory the artificial atmosphere of a close green-house, when the sun is full upon it. Such mornings in Bombay are called *muggy*, and are always the forerunners of extreme heat. You are prepared for this unhealthy evaporation, which is often very dense towards the close of this season, by putting on a flannel jacket; having the fear of rheumatism, or country-ague before your eyes; disorders from which, in consequence of imprudent exposure to the many atmospheric changes that assail the European in India, all, more or less, suffer severely. There is an indescribable sweetness in the morning at this hour; (six o'clock.) It is as if every leaf and flower, nay, the very earth itself, were exhaling some delicious perfume wherewith to refresh you, and offering up an early tribute to the Giver of all good for the past night's refreshing dews, which still glitter in diamond globules around you. Vegetation does rejoice, for it has been revived and nourished; and the pores of its leaves are freed from dust by these gentle distillations that fall from heaven, unseen by man. Night-dews on this island are very heavy; and I have often been surprised upon returning home between nine and ten of an evening to find my clothes wet and uncomfortable from this cause, though the atmosphere at the time was clear and serene. With the breaking forth of the sun the mist vanishes, and the loveliest of all hours bursts upon the world. Soon, however, the leaves of many of the trees and shrubs begin gradually to droop, so as to offer as small a surface as possible to his withering rays: I was often struck with this singular phenomenon, which we cannot look upon but as a beautiful provision for the protection of plants at mid-day. During these comparatively cool hours, there blossom numbers of garden and wild flowers, whose beauty before noon has faded and gone. Butterflies, and a host of minor honey-sucking insects are now on the wing, seeking, while the calix that offers it yet lives, their morning's repast, and flitting about like bright meteors; till, having satisfied their wants, they retire to the shade of some thick grove, there to slumber till the sun sinks low, and fresh blossoms open to them their evening nectaries. Now may be seen the large tree-lizard, remarkable for the curious pouch under his head, very busy and alert, springing from branch to branch, and pouncing upon the poor flies driven into his domain by the ascending sun; his hour has now arrived, and he must breakfast while opportunity offers. There is another pretty saurian, which also claims our attention; and which has often afforded me amusement of a morning from seven o'clock until nine. He is very swift on his little feet, and is compactly and elegantly formed; having a fine brown shining skin beautifully mottled. He has no pouch like the former; is about fourteen inches in length when full grown; his favourite haunts appear to be in old walls, or under the thatch or tiles of your bungalow; here you may spy him from beneath the arch formed by the half tile, peeping cautiously out with two very bright and sharp eyes, watching, like his tree, neighbour, for any stray insects that may be tempted to creep in under the roof for shelter and protection from the sun. If he is not successful in his sport, he steals out occasionally from his hiding-place, and you are surprised to see so small a head in conjunction with so long a body. If the tiles are not too hot for his feet, he looks about him anxiously, as if he had been decoyed into some unfavourable position, which he wanted to change; but the least noise disturbs him; even a bird flying past will cause him to dart into another opening under the roof, and in a second or two the bright little eyes are again detected, for he is still hungry. I made several attempts to secure a specimen of this lizard, but was always unsuccessful. Not so with the tree-lizards; of them I caught many for examination, by simply passing a loop or running knot made of twine, and attached to the end of a long bamboo, over their heads, and thus bringing them down from the bough on which they were roosting, often to the amusement of the *molly* or gardener, who appeared to take a lively interest in the sport, as soon as he found that I did not capture them for any cruel purpose. Both species are very harmless, as indeed are all the lizard tribe; but when crushed or irritated in the hand, they would endeavour to liberate themselves by trying to bite me. They have little power over the muscles of the lower jaw. Like all other reptiles in the East, they both have numerous enemies; and are thus prevented from multiplying to a troublesome extent. The large kites in their mornings' circuits do not consider them beneath their notice; and their young ones are devoured by frogs and snakes. The *Zootoca Vivipara*, or nimble lizard, so common in summer on our heaths and sunny banks at home, is not unlike the bungalow lizard, though much smaller. They both bring forth their young *alive;* the eggs being hatched while yet in the body of the parent; consequently they are *ovo-viviparous.* The vivifying heat of the sun is thought to be necessary for the extrusion of the young from the eggs. I kept a female that had been caught for me, some weeks in a small box covered with a glass lid, and was not a little surprised one morning, when I went to give her the usual allowance of flies, to see five or six young ones running about and tumbling over their mother. Though but a few hours old, they readily seized the imprisoned insects, and ate them up so rapidly, that the parent stood but a poor chance amongst them. Snakes are not very common on the south side of the Island of Bombay; I only saw two or three during my residence there, though I often hunted for them in the old thorny spurge or Euporbia hedges. The study of animated nature always afforded me the greatest pleasure; and India, where all to me was novel and strange, opened a tempting field for its pursuit. Our servants, well knowing the haunts of these reptiles, would occasionally kill one in the compound early in the morning; while rather torpid after the cold night, they lay coiled up under the shrubs. The natives are very expert in killing the most venomous snakes, and really seem to be more terrified by the sight of some of them than even strangers are. As the Coolies, and many of the poor people go barefooted, they travel over the waste lands with great caution; and practise has given them a quickness of eye in detecting snakes on the ground. As they creep out of their hiding places after dark, and ramble about in search of mice and insects, no one thinks of going out without a lantern, and an attendant with a stout stick, who walks before, and carefully marks the road if an unfrequented one. This of course is only necessary in country places. The cobra de capello, and the bright speckled cobra manilla, are not uncommon on the north and west sides of the island; and many of the private gardens that are densely crowded with shrubs and flowering plants, are said to be infested at particular seasons by a small brown snake. An officer, on sick-leave, who was residing in one of the government bungalows at Colabah, about a mile from the Fort of Bombay, was walking up and down one morning under the verandah in a pair of thin slippers, and accidentally trod upon a small snake that was winding itself out of a hole in his path. Within a few minutes afterwards he was seized by the most violent pain in his foot, which soon changed colour, and swelled up enormously to the knee. Sickness, and convulsions, with the usual symptoms of having been poisoned, rapidly appeared; and medical aid was immediately resorted to, but nothing could arrest the progress of the fatal virus. Castor-oil, and other native remedies, were useless here; and the poor gentleman expired in dreadful agonies twenty-four hours after he had been bitten. The fangs of the snake, as it is unnecessary to say, had easily penetrated the flimsy slipper; thus showing the danger of going out in India with a thin covering over the feet. This officer died from the bite of a small snake, known as the carpet snake, from the circumstance of its often creeping into rooms, and hiding under the matting. The carpet snake or cobra minilla is, I believe, one of the most poisonous and subtle reptiles found in the island, and is very difficult to detect in the long and withered grasses.

Turning from these formidable and life-destroying enemies, which, in certain districts, excite such a feeling of horror from their numbers, and which have become objects of veneration and worship to many of the tribes and castes of India, we will now make a few passing remarks on some other very common and troublesome insects, that alarm the visitor more from their loathsome aspect, than from any power which they possess of inflicting a mortal wound. The scorpion is one of the dreaded inhabitants of Bombay, but it does not attain that large size so peculiar to Africa and the West Indies. It frequents the old ruined bungalows, cotton stores, and other unoccupied buildings; and many of the native coasting vessels, from the nature of their cargo, are said to be often infested by it. The scorpions I have seen in Bombay were of a reddish or dirty yellow hue. They creep into godowns, and cellars, and wage a mortal war with the long-legged spiders already spoken of. As they are very prolific, and bring forth at a birth fifty or sixty young ones, it is highly necessary to have a proper person occasionally to purify these haunts, so as to prevent them from increasing upon your premises. They inflict with their armed tail a wound which, in irritable and nervous subjects, is often attended by unpleasant symptoms; and I have heard of one or two instances in which death ensued from the poison of the malignant sting of an old scorpion; but if I remember correctly, the victims in these cases were in a bad state of health. During a short sojourn in Guzerat, a distressing event of this kind, which occurs to my recollection, took place at one of the military stations. A soldier's wife had brought in some clothes that had been placed out near the barracks in the sun to dry, and having carelessly thrown them upon a bed, she took up a child that was crying in a cradle to quiet it with the breast; and, after hushing it to sleep, laid it upon the bed where the clothes were deposited. In a few minutes the child's screams aroused the mother, when, upon examination, she discovered that she had placed her sleeping babe upon a scorpion, that had been concealed in the clothes. The army surgeon was immediately sent for, but the child expired a short time after his arrival.

The genus scolopendra, or centipede, is another very common and troublesome insect in Bombay; indeed, in some parts of the country, centipedes are so numerous, that the inhabitants are obliged to put the feet of their bed-posts in water to prevent these crawling creatures from lodging themselves in the mattress—a place in which they are fond of breeding. Like the scorpion, they move about in dark and unfrequented places, and issue forth at night in search of food. I had always an instinctive dread of this insect—more so, I really believe, than any other; and can remember, upon my first arrival in Bombay, the precaution I took to guard against them—never putting on a boot, shoe, or glove, without first shaking or carefully examining it. We have all our particular dislikes to one kind of moving creature or another. Some faint at the sight of a spider—

others at a harmless blue-bottle—I, myself, being terrified beyond measure at the appearance of a centipede, however small. These centipedes inflict a painful, and to young children, a most dangerous wound. A labourer once allowed me to examine his index finger, which had been stung by a centipede while removing some old timber; and the flesh of which had shrivelled up and appeared like dry parchment stretched over the bone. He had ligamentous anchylosis of the first and second joints. The whole finger was of course useless to him, and ought to have been removed; but the poor fellow could never make up his mind to the operation. The first centipede which I saw was in rather a strange place. It fell from the bottom of a dinner-plate that was handed to me at table, but was crushed and dead. As the Hindoo servants *will* place everything on the floor in the cooking-house, though they have tables provided, it was easy to account for the unwelcome presence of this horrid insect. The centipede grows to five or six inches in length, and, from the number of its legs, is enabled to move very quickly. The hymenopterous insects, such as hornets, wasps, and bees, are very numerous on this and the neighbouring islands. They form their cells in the old trees and excavations of Elephanta and Salsette, and hang in immense clusters from the roofs of these subterranean temples. Some of the hornets are of a large size, and often spread terror among the toddy-drawers in the palm-tope by swarming around the trees they have to ascend during the process of tapping.

The inferior inhabitants of the fields and woods in India appear to shun the heat of the mid-day sun, as much as man does. It is seldom that you see a bird flying about at this hour, unless it be the large kite or fulvous vulture held sacred by the Hindoos, and protected and encouraged by the English as the natural scavenger of the town and country. He cares little about the heat; for he can keep his thinly feathered body cool by the fanning of his powerful wings. These birds are very tame, and will often sit close to your cook while he is preparing your dinner, and watch anxiously for any stray morsels which that functionary may be pleased to bestow upon them; appearing, from the regularity of their hours of attendance, to have a very good idea of time. They usually announce their arrival by half a dozen loud and shrill notes, uttered at intervals as they sweep round your compound, and finally perch themselves on the roof of an outbuilding, or the topmost branch of a tree, where, if the day is very hot, they spread out their wings and keep up a gentle motion with them on the principle of a fan. Your Portuguese servants, if not prevented, often amuse themselves by setting, near their resting-places, a rat-trap, baited with a piece of meat, which is soon pounced upon by these unconscious birds, who then find themselves caught by the leg between the teeth of this cruel instrument. The Portuguese domestics annoy in this way some Hindoo servant to whom they owe a grudge, and upon whom they wish to revenge themselves, by thus destroying the birds which the Hindoos venerate. Shoot them, they dare not; since the report of the gun would draw the attention of their master or of the police, who would immediately have the offenders punished. In every town throughout the East you meet with these useful birds; indeed, they have evidently been created for the benefit of mankind in that country. Were it not for their services, the air in that hot climate would be constantly tainted by the decaying of animal matter, so injurious to human health; and their keen eyes, and fine sense of smell, enable them to discover at a great distance the dead animals on which they feed. I have counted more than twenty of these kites at a time upon the body of a kid, at the distance of several miles from any village. The jackals, however, had first had their share. The woods, at this season, are alive with the smaller birds, which keep up an incessant din with their chattering and squabbling; but excepting the cooing of the turtle doves, and the occasional familiar note of the Indian cuckoo, which is more sonorous than our migratory bird, there are but few that remind us of the sweet songsters of our own English groves. Nature, however, in this respect, may be said to distribute her favours and gifts equally; since the richness of plumage which distinguishes many of these tropical birds compensates, in a great measure, for the loss of a musical voice. Splendid, indeed, is the apparel of numbers of them; but the various species most remarkable for brilliancy of plumage have been nearly exterminated on the Island of Bombay by the English, and their unerring Joe Manton's. I have, in my rambles, noticed the small kingfisher, (Alcedo Asiatica,) a bird bearing a strong resemblance to our own solitary species; indeed, I might say identical with it. Another of this genus about the size of a missel thrush, frequented some trees that shaded a tank in our compound. The back, wings, and tail feathers were of the most splendid azure, and the head and body of a rich brown, shot with purple—throat white, bill and feet red. The swallow-tailed emerald fly-catchers were very common in the rocky districts above Malabar point; and some small green woodpeckers, with crimson and yellow throats, were often heard and seen by me tapping the dead trees about Parel. I have also seen here the Malabar shrike, (Lanius Malabaricus, Lath;) hoopoe, (Upupa epops;) sand-piper, (Tringa hypoleucos;) common house sparrow, (Fringilla domestica, Linn;) tree sparrow, (Fringilla montana, Linn;) and a variety of birds common to Great Britain; but space does not admit of my enumerating more of them here. It is greatly to be lamented, that hundreds of these beautiful island-birds are annually most wantonly destroyed by the crews of European ships for the sake of a few bright feathers; though seldom, I fear, to enrich the cabinet of the true naturalist, or effectively to further the study of Indian ornithology. Since it is not the design of this work to illustrate the Fauna of Bombay and its neighbourhood, beyond simply giving the reader, just as occasion may offer, an outline or idea of some of its various members, we will now turn for the present to other matters of history more immediately connected with that lord of the creation, Man, and take a peep at him as he appears at Bombay, at home, and abroad.

CHAPTER VI.

"Oh! for one draught of cooling northern air
That it might pour its freshness on me now;
That it might kiss my cheek and cleave my hair,
And part its currents round my fever'd brow."

The Hot season. Depressing days. Anglo Indians. Change of air necessary. Good effects of sea voyage to invalids. Children born in India. Their separation from their parents. Necessity of exercise. Arungzebe. A Hindoo's idea of happiness. The poor obliged to rise early. Washing at the tanks. Bitter beer and spirit drinking. Dangers of exposure to the sun. Good example of the natives. How to ward off sickness. Flannel valuable in warm climates. Luxury of a cold bath. Sleepy servants. Give your dogs Exercise. The blessed morning breeze. Tiffin. Dress coats and white jackets. Dancing. The Horse-hair Jupe. Dinner parties and their miseries. Wages of domestics. Cooks and cookery. English dishes. Preserved meats. How to make a fortune. Porous jars and wine coolers. Duties of the Abdar. Indian hospitality. Boarding houses, &c., &c.

It would be a difficult task to convey to the reader a correct idea of the prostrating effect of some of the dreadfully hot days which, during an Indian sojourn, you have but too often to endure, with what share of patience and resignation you may be blessed withal.

It has indeed been asserted, that, in a year or two, you become accustomed, and in fact *acclimatized* to the heated temperature, and care but little about the burning seasons as they roll; but I must say, that many of the old Anglo-Indians, whom I had the pleasure of knowing during my short residence amongst them, (some of them of twenty years standing in the country,) one and all asserted, that so far from becoming accustomed to the heat by degrees, they found that every year brought fresh trials to the constitution, until, at last, though not suffering from any organic disease, they were compelled to seek a change of air, either at the Cape of Good Hope, or in their native country. This change from a relaxing to a bracing air is looked upon as absolutely necessary every four or five years, in order to ensure to a European resident in India even a moderate share of that greatest of all blessings, health. 'Tis true, there are sanitary stations in the hilly districts of India, to which every year, in the hot season, numbers fly who can obtain a month or two's leave of absence; but the enormous expense of travelling deprives many a poor ensign or lieutenant, perhaps encumbered with a family, of the power of taking advantage of their fine temperature. The effect of a sea voyage, as a restorative in cases of general debility, is wonderful; so marvellously does the enfeebled system begin to revive as the ship enters into cooler regions, and draws near to the lofty mountains that look down upon Table Bay—particularly if the voyage takes place about June or July, about which time the winter quarter there sets in. Sick officers who required a sea voyage were formerly allowed to proceed to the Cape to recruit their health, perhaps for a year, when they would not have been permitted to return home.— Now, however, the regulations are, I believe, altered; as it would take nearly the same time to go to the Cape by ship, that would be required to reach England by the present overland route. Children born in India are, generally speaking, poor, puny, sickly little things. Hundreds of them languish and die, during the first or second year of their brief existence.— Some, indeed, through extraordinary care and good nursing, outlive the period of infancy; but unless they are sent home at the age of seven or eight years, their lives are rarely prolonged to old age; it is not solely with a view to their education that Indian-born children are separated at an early age from their parents, and sent to England. This separation is a dreadful trial to the poor parents. Mothers, in particular, appear to love, with an affection doubly ardent, the children who, in a foreign clime, are the solace of their often weary exile. Every morning, before sunrise, the picturesque sea-shores and public drives on the island are crowded by a motley company of visitors in search of health and exercise. As this is the only portion of the day, during the hot season, in which you can really walk with any comfort or advantage, every one, who can, avails himself of it for an hour or two's stroll before breakfast, either on foot or on horseback; and an improved appetite, and greater willingness to undertake the ordinary duties of the day, bear witness to the beneficial effects of the practice. By following up the custom regularly, you certainly avoid much of that dreadful lassitude and sense of weariness which oppresses those of your less resolute English neighbours, who pass in their beds those delightful hours which they ought to spend in the bracing morning air. Were early out-of-door exercise more practised than it is, we should see but few wasting upon couches the best portion of their lives, in listless inactivity; and giving way to that infectious indolence, which, as the parent of one half of our diseases, cannot be too resolutely resisted, and which grows so imperceptibly by indulgence. May we not learn, from the page of history, to trace the misery and slavery, which has been entailed on India, to the careless, sensual, and effeminate habits of its original possessors? Aurungzebe, indeed, when he invaded it, at once understood the character of the aborigines; and by constant watchfulness guarded his followers, during a period of thirty years, from the fatal though seductive influence of climate and example; but his successors soon fell an easy prey to indolence and luxury; their splendour and power passed away from them; and these Mohammedan conquerors sank, if possible, lower in the scale of humanity than even their Hindoo subjects.

It has been thought that the approach of death is contemplated with less terror by the natives of India than by those of any other country in the world.—This may possibly arise from the Hindoo belief, that a state of perfect tranquillity is the summit of happiness; and that to deaden the ever-active principle of life within us—that living principle which animated the dust of the earth when God breathed into Adam's nostrils the breath of life, and man became a living soul—must be the great desire of all. "It is better to sleep than to be active," say they; "but death is the best state of all; for then the daily care of the body ceases to trouble us, and the future shall be to us an endless sleep; a vacuum where no sound disturbs." This theory would seem, in India, to be practically followed up by the rich, who may in truth be said to sleep away a third part of their short lives; and who resort to a thousand plans in order to bring about this desirable end. As I have already observed, they chew opium; and the juice of an intoxicating substance prepared from a species of hemp, and called *beng*, or *bhang*, is in common use among them.—*Cherris*, another vegetable narcotic of this class, esteemed as "the leaf of delusion," is taken as we would take wine, for the pleasurable feelings it excites, though often producing insanity. Their rooms are darkened, and the softest and most luxurious couches and rugs are distributed about the apartment, as if to court sleep. With the poor, however, who *fortunately* have to labour for their daily food, it is otherwise. They are all early risers, and at peep of day you may see swarms of them collected around the large public tanks, taking their shower-baths, by dexterously swinging a vessel of water over their heads, and refreshing themselves in a variety of ways peculiar to the East. Numbers of poor persons also frequent these tanks at this hour, to wash their linen; remaining, till their garments are dried and fit to put on again, up to their necks in the water. Evening again brings crowds around these water-cisterns, to fill their *chattees* for domestic purposes. In some of these respects the natives set us a good example. I myself know, by experience, how great an effort it is to rise early in India; and many a battle have I had, to conquer self, and get up and sally forth, when aroused at gunfire. Often, during the night, the heat is so great, even in the best planned bungalows, that to sleep is impossible; the drowsy god refuses to visit your couch, and morning dawns ere your eyelids close. Nevertheless, the man, who in India is anxious to preserve his health, *must* be an early riser. He must also, as he will quickly learn, avoid the vile habit of drinking bitter beer at all hours—a practice no more necessary in India than England, yet very fashionable in Indian society. The strictest temperance, with great simplicity of diet, is here necessary. Spirituous liquors of course must be avoided; and if, in seasons of langour and depression, wine must be taken, let it be the best that can be procured, and not the light, sour stuff, which, imported in immense quantities, is swallowed wholesale, because it is thought to be harmless. Let the European also avoid all unnecessary exposure to the sun; for though he may be able to bear its heat with but little inconvenience, such exposure, particularly to the newly arrived, is injurious in the extreme. Even the natives acknowledge its danger, and guard against it by every means in their power. The poorest native will not venture out in the daytime, without his chittree over his head, although the head is already well protected by the ample folds of the white turban, which cannot absorb many of the sun's rays, and within which, as an extra security, many persons put large green leaves, which they gather fresh for the purpose every morning, and which must be cool and grateful to their shaven craniums. Those of our countrymen who are liable to attacks of dysentery, or to complaints of the liver, are always recommended to wear, during the rainy season, a flannel roller, to protect that important and often-deranged organ; and flannel vests are considered necessary all the year through. These few hints may perhaps not prove unacceptable to some of my readers whose lot may one day be cast in India.—None of us can tell what a year, nay, what a day may bring forth; our life is made up of strange adventures, and we know not what may be on the morrow.

The first object to which your desires point upon getting up of a morning, are a cup of tea or coffee and a bath. The latter is certainly the greatest of luxuries, if you can, by any natural or artificial means, cool the water sufficiently to produce a reviving shock. Many persons, I am aware, condemn the very cold bath, and prefer the tepid; in fact, the cold bath, during my stay in Bombay, fell into disrepute in consequence of two or three deaths, which occurred during its actual use. I believe, however, that the deaths of the supposed victims of these baths were occasioned by their imprudently plunging into very cold water when overheated by exercise. By eight o'clock the sun has risen too high, and become too oppressive, to allow any European to remain longer out of doors. All at home, too, by this time, are ready for breakfast; and if your *Molly* is a clever gardener, the table is not only graced by sweet flowers, but by delicious fruits; both of which must always be acceptable. Your sitting-rooms have undergone a change; every door and window is darkened by the wet *cuscus* mats (tatties) which, during your absence, have been suspended in front of them. The large flounced centre punkah floats monotonously from the ceiling; and your many servants begin already to look drowsy and stupid, and are anxious to get out of sight, and to take their accustomed nap as soon as possible in some quiet corner of your bungalow. If you are fond of keeping dogs, your *sycee*, or groom, will sometimes condescend to look after them in kennel; the *chokra*, or message-boy, having to take them out every morning, all fastened together, for a walk. You meet dozens of these boys on the sea-shore, each with their string of dogs; some running races with them, or teaching them tricks; but others sitting still, or, as is often the case, sleeping, with the cord tied round their waist, to prevent the dogs from running away. About eleven o'clock the sea-breeze sets in; and, though out of doors, this breeze is hot and furnace-like, the temperature of your apartments, as the blessed current passes into them, is lowered considerably; and, about one o'clock, you can sit down, and enjoy your luncheon or tiffin. Tiffin, in India, is a most agreeable repast; seeing that it does not take place till all formal visiting is over for the day. The talkative and the inquisitive visitors have, before this happy hour, gone through their various and well-known evolutions, and have mercifully left you once more alone with your family, or with the really valued friend; a treasure often difficult to be found in any country; and the remainder of the day is at your own disposal. The English in Bombay dine usually at seven o'clock. This gives them an hour or two's drive before dinner; but eight o'clock is the hour for fashionable parties, and you are fortunate if you get anything to eat before half-past. Coffee is handed round soon after the cloth is drawn, and but little wine is drunk; a great change in this respect having taken place during the last fifteen or twenty years. Formerly, drinking was one of the crying evils of our countrymen in the East; and, together with gambling and other seductive vices, was the ruin of our young officers there; but now, a man who either drinks or games, is cut as a public nuisance, and shunned by every one who has the least pretensions to respectability. Gentlemen who pay visits, are expected to do so in dress cloth coats, or full regimentals, as the case may be. This regulation may not appear very remarkable to English readers; but the fact is, that to wear a woollen coat in India during the hot season for three or four hours together in a crowded room, is an amount of misery rather difficult for a person at home to conceive. So ridiculous a custom cannot be too much condemned; for pleasure is thus in a great measure destroyed, and, in some cases, even apoplexy is induced by this stupid fashion, which all sober-thinking people abhor. At parties where ladies are not present, the host (if a reasonable being) will sometimes request his guests to put on their white linen jackets, which they generally take good care to bring with them in the drawer of their palanquin in case they should be wanted. The fair sex, in consequence of their style of dress, do not suffer half so much as the gentlemen. With them the hoop, and horse-hair jupe, are in great request, and balloon out the thin muslin, or China satin, in a manner which, as I could fancy, must be very agreeable; but these spreading garments have their disadvantages; they fill up a room; and if waltzing, &c., be introduced, (for such things are verily done in India, in spite of the thermometer indicating 100 degrees,) none but a gentleman with a very long arm has the slightest chance of reaching gracefully the narrow zone of his Elizabethan partner. I am not surprised that the Asiatics laugh at us for *taking the trouble*, as they say, to dance, when, for a few rupees, we could hire pretty nautch-girls to do the whole for us; but Englishmen are fond of keeping up English customs, and may be forgiven for thus amusing themselves in a foreign land. Whenever you dine out, you must take your own servant to wait upon you at table, or you have a very poor chance of procuring anything like a satisfactory dinner. This is another nuisance; for should your room be small, you have as many servants as friends in it; for the servants attend to none but their own employers. These people quite delight in the bustle and stir of a large party; and all come dressed up in a nondescript-kind of livery, according to the fancy, humour, or pride of their masters. The only articles they retain of their own, are the turban and turned-up slippers; the latter of which often give rise to some ludicrous scenes of confusion. Should two or three guests take a fancy to the same dish at the same time, a race to the carver is not very unusual; for the native attendants are always anxious to appear sharp and active on such occasions; and they not unfrequently hook one another with the aforesaid turned up slippers, and come floundering to the ground. They keep up a perpetual jabbering in Hindostanee, behind your chairs; and as they chew betel-nut, garlic, and some other horrible compounds, they do not add much to the comfort of your dinner table on a sultry evening. Yet there is something very picturesque and pretty in the dress of these Hindoo servants. One man will have on a splendid orange-coloured robe, another a crimson one, another a purple, and so on; and their turbans are snowy white, and often fringed with a drooping gold-lace border, or have silver-thread woven into them.

The lower orders of the Portuguese are much employed by English families, as cooks and butlers; for the Hindoos are useless as culinary servants, from their peculiar religious feelings about food. Nothing could persuade a Hindoo to touch ham, bacon, or butchers' meat. Without exception, I should say, that the Portuguese cooks are the most troublesome people you have to deal with in India. They are constantly intoxicated; and many of them are monstrous thieves. They think nothing of going away on some excursion of pleasure, for three or four days, and leaving you to get your dinners cooked as you best can, or go without any; for none of your other dozen servants will render you the least assistance, and would rather quit your service than touch anything connected with the cook's department. Servants are the pests of India, for you live in constant danger of being robbed; and, I should fancy, that a day seldom elapses in which you are not robbed in one way or another. The only way you can possibly get on with them is, by constantly threatening to send them to the bazaar master, and have them punished; or by withholding their pay. Their wages vary from ten shillings to thirty shillings per month, in Bombay, according to their duties and stations; but one great blessing is, you have no trouble in supplying them with food, and their wages cover all demands. They sleep outside, in the verandah, or in some passage or lobby during the rainy season; and, with all their faults and imperfections, it is astonishing how soon you get attached to them. Many of them are married; and when that is the case, you allow them to erect a hut in your compound to live in; and, as they set forth their meals upon the floor, simply spreading out a piece of matting, they require very little furniture. A bedstead, a box or two, and half a dozen different sized brass and earthen chatties, or cooking-pots; and half a cocoanut filled with oil, and a cottton wick, lights up their simple room at night. They make a fire in a corner, between two or three stones, to boil their rice and curry, which is the principal food they live upon. Of course, the cook and his Portuguese assistants have nothing to do with them. He lives and sleeps in the bobbergy-house, or kitchen; but he is always on good terms with the other servants; and it is very seldom that your domestic comfort is broken in upon by fights or quarrels amongst them. Each man has his particular duty to perform in your house. The lady of the establishment never interferes with anything. Your cook is called in after breakfast, and told what to purchase for the day, and what to prepare for dinner, which he cooks to perfection; for they are celebrated for their made-dishes and curries.—You seldom see what he has purchased, till it is on the table. At night you enquire the cost. You are, in consequence, never troubled with green-grocers', butchers', or other bills of this description, coming in at Christmas, as everything in the way of food is paid for when ordered; a happy system that would work well at home—benefiting not only the creditor by ready money payments, which would enable him to sell his goods the cheaper, but the debtor, by the pleasing thought of owing no man anything. To return, however, to the dinner-table. It appears to be the great ambition of all dinner-party givers in India to have as many English dishes on the table as possible. The hermetically sealed meats, soups, and confections, that are sent out in tin cases, and principally manufactured in Glasgow for the Indian market, are in high repute in Bombay; and it is curious to sit down and dine upon Scotch salmon, or turbot, as fresh as if but just caught in its native stream; or to partake of a dish of green peas, or carrots, grown in the land of cakes. Green gooseberries, currants, rhubarb, and other bottled fruits, are much used in pastry, and, though excessively dear, the bazaars are seldom over-stocked, as the very dearness of these articles has made them fashionable. Stilton, and other celebrated cheeses are sent out in lead cases, but soon become dry and hard; and if not carefully watched, fall a prey to creeping things innumerable; even these leaden cases are not always proof against the adamantine teeth of the bandecoote, or country rat, that infests your store-rooms and larders. I remember being presented with a fragment of oaten cake, a package of which had been sent overland, as a great treat, to some friends in Bombay, though its carriage must have cost, at least, a rupee an ounce. Miniature fountains, playing in crystal basons filled with the choicest flowers, are occasionally seen on the tables of some of the merchant-princes of the East; in fact, every plan that is calculated to cool the atmosphere of their suffocating rooms, is adopted. I have often thought that, if any man in this age of wonders, were fortunate enough to hit upon an invention that would lower the temperature of these heated apartments in the hot season, to 70 or 72 deg., he would make his fortune in twelve months, and be loaded with honours as lasting as those which have been heaped even upon a Nelson, or a Wellington. Man's ingenuity has certainly been put to the test here; and not without some desirable results. He has called in chemistry to his assistance; and attraction and repulsion have been duly investigated. Every known refrigerant has had its day, and even the ice that covers the great American lakes has found its way into the wine-coolers of the Anglo-Indian. Porous jars of common country-ware, are very well adapted for cooling water. They are generally made of a fine clay, and as they are not glazed, the water slowly percolates through the sides, and the consequent evaporation cools the fluid within. They are commonly suspended by a cane-work handle to the under branch of a tree near your bungalow.

Some cover them, as they do also vessels containing wine, beer, &c., with a bag dipt into a solution of muriate of ammonia, nitrate of potash, salt, and water; thus producing in fact, a freezing mixture. One of the great disputes between the Abdar, (water-cooler,) and his master, turns upon the neglect of this really important duty; for you can drink nothing in India until it has been properly cooled. This cooling process certainly causes no small trouble in a large family, for your servants are constantly losing your cooling bags, and cannot comprehend their utility. Much has been said of Indian hospitality; and, generally speaking, an Englishman is pretty certain of a hearty welcome, when he arrives in the country, if he has the least introduction to any English family in the place; and this may account, in some manner, for the absence of boarding-houses in Bombay; as there is only one that has the least pretensions to that name in the Fort: I believe this is the case in Calcutta. Captains of vessels usually sleep on board their ships in harbour; and cadets and officers, upon landing in India, have quarters immediately provided for them; so it is only the unknown adventurer who feels the want of an hotel, when cast lonely upon the ancient shores of Hindostan.

CHAPTER VII.

> "Together let us beat this ample field,
> Try what the open, what the covert yield;
> The latent tracts, the giddy heights, explore
> Of all who blindly creep, or sightless soar;
> Eye Nature's walks, shoot folly as it flies,
> And catch the manners living as they rise."

How Englishmen lose caste. Expense of Palanquins and travelling. Hindoo gentlemen. Variety of characters. Religious rank and distinction. Feasts and festivals. Bagabatee and Doorga. Native holidays. Kartek and Ganesh. The fate of a Goddess. Infant betrothments. The mystic fire. Frightful monstrosities. The darkness of the Hindoos. Peep at the Esplanade. Tents of the Commander-in-Chief. Bands of music. Portable houses. Singular wandering people. A drunken English sailor, his fate. Disadvantages of living in tents. The power of a hungry musquitoe. Tipula Plumicornis. The prayers on the sea shore. Arabian Jew. Devout Parsees. England's ten talents. What can we do individually. Have we done our duty to India. Worthy bishops. The Presidency of Bombay. Its extent and population. Mount Meru, &c., &c.

PECUNIARY circumstances would not always admit of my keeping a *tattoo*, or palanquin, so my out-door exercise depended, in a great measure, upon the use I might make of my own legs; and though it is thought extremely vulgar to be seen walking anywhere, and you are supposed to lose *caste* by the first offence of this kind perpetrated in public, yet was I vulgar enough to walk every day; and truly if we allow such trifling matters as these to disturb our happiness, we can expect but a sorry pilgrimage in the vale through which all of us must wend our way. Few can form an idea what enormous sums of money are annually expended in India in palanquin hire alone, by people who are fearful of being thought poor, or are too proud to walk short distances. I remember one individual, whose salary was only eighty rupees a month, and out of which he actually paid twenty to be carried half a mile twice a-day, to and from his place of business, by four bearers. My poverty in this case was, perhaps, an advantage to me; for, gentle reader, I am not ashamed to confess, that I *was* poor in India; it gave me a better opportunity of extending my knowledge of the country, and of observing the national character of the people, with whom it was my lot to be mixed up in their daily avocations, and of studying the habits and customs of this large portion of the great human family, now living under the happy rule of Great Britain. There is something extremely pleasing and winning in the natives. The Hindoo gentleman is polite, affable, and agreeable, though to those unaccustomed to Oriental salutations, his address may at times rather savour of servility. He entertains a high opinion of the English. His dress is very plain and simple, consisting of a close-fitting robe and full trowsers; and though the possessor of two or three lacks of rupees, he makes as low a salaam to you as the poor hard-working *coolie*, who vegetates on a few pice a day, and lies down at night, contented and happy, under an old mat stretched over a few bamboos. Differing so much as they do in religious matters, it is truly surprising to find in Bombay such a large number of men peaceably engaged in the great pursuit of the mammon of this world. Here are Jews, Turks, Portuguese, Armenians, Parsees, Arabians, Hindoos, and an endless variety of *castes*, all quietly living together, yet apart, respecting and obeying the powers that be. No one interferes with his neighbour, in matters connected with his faith. All religions are tolerated; and the Christian missionary, in order to gain a convert, has an arduous work to perform, and a thousand obstacles with which to contend. The history of the castes of India, no doubt, is familiar to many of my readers; but as it is probable, that this little volume may fall into the hands of young persons not yet conversant with Indian subjects, I shall, as I have already done, give occasionally short sketches of what has been gleaned from the fabled accounts handed down in the sacred writings of the East, so as to blend instruction with amusement. The word "caste," like many others in use in India, is a Portuguese word (*casta*), which signifies a race or lineage. These castes, of which there is now such an infinite variety, are said to have originally consisted of four orders. The Indian sacred books tell us, that the Brahmins, who compose the first order, proceeded directly from the *mouth* of the Creator, the seat of wisdom; the Cshatriaya, from his *arm;* the Vaisya, from his *thigh;* and the Sudra, from his *heel.* The Brahmins were priests, or holy men; the Cshatriaya, soldiers, or fighting men; the Vaisyas, tillers of the land, or husbandmen; and the Sudras, servants, or daily labourers. In Mr. Mills' work we learn, that all the impure castes which have sprung from these are to be ascribed to the force of circumstances which laws could not reach; while the children born of parents of different castes were regarded as belonging to no caste at all—their unfortunate birth sinking them beneath the degraded Sudra. These castes, in time, became a formidable body; and the sacred books state, that the Brahmins, by supernatural means, *created* a Sovereign, to arrest the growing evil. This wonderful person classified them, and gave to each a particular occupation; and instead of thieves and robbers, they became industrious artisans. Thirty-six classes are there spoken of; but their actual numbers are not known. I have mingled with the enormous population that covers the small Island of Bombay—a population amounting to 566,119 souls, without its dependencies, and have been a passive spectator of their festivals, unrivalled perhaps in their attractive splendour. One of the most striking of these festivals is the Doorga poojah, which is annually held in Bombay, and which, commencing on the 15th of October, continues for three or four days. It is held in honour of a female already introduced to us at the caves of Elephanta, as the slayer of the terrible giant Parvati. A very splendid image of her is constructed; and after various ceremonies, the Brahmins, on the third day, touch different parts of the idol set up to Bhagabatee, for such is her title in Bombay, and then publicly declare, that the departed spirit of Bhagabatee has come into her. The consequence of this farce is, that hundreds, firmly believing in all this nonsense, bring costly gifts to the shrine; all of which are quietly taken possession of by the grave priests (quite a Popish trick). But I shall quote Malcom's graphic description of this festival, as he witnessed it in Calcutta, where holidays of this sort are carried on with greater zest than in Bombay, and are better supported by the rich Hindoo population, who can always find plenty of money to expend in religious follies of this sort. He says, "The first day is spent in waking up Doorga, and other gods, who are supposed to have slept since the festival of Shayan Ekadashee. The second day, vows are made, and offerings of water, flowers, sweetmeats, &c., are presented. The third day is occupied with ceremonies to bring the soul of Doorga into the image. To effect this, the priest repeats prayers, offers incantations, and touches the eyes, cheeks, nose, breast, &c., of the image with his finger. The image now becomes an object of worship, and crowds offer it divine honours, presenting at the same time large quantities of fruits, clothing, and food, which, of course, are perquisites to the Brahmins. The fourth day streams with the blood of animal sacrifices. The worshippers dance before the idol, smeared with gore; drums beat, and shouts rend the air. The heads only of the victims are offered, the worshippers eating the carcases, and rioting in strong drink. Such Hindoos as worship Vishnu, not being permitted to shed blood, offer pumpkins, melons, sugar-cane, &c., which are cut in two with the sacrificial knife, that the juice may flow forth. All these days the image is kept in the house, and the services performed in inferior courts, so that the streets show little of confusion or stir. The evenings are occupied with songs and dancing, often of an indecent character."

The author goes on to say, that "the last and great day brings the goddess abroad, carried in triumph upon the shoulders of men, to be thrown into the river." In Bombay, Bhagabatee was taken down to Back Bay, but not thrown into the sea. The procession here extended for nearly half a mile—one of the most interesting I ever remember seeing in India. The splendid holiday attire of the natives, each one carrying a rich-coloured umbrella, or some little mimic temple containing a wax figure, about the size of a Dutch doll—children glittering in cloth of gold and jewels—cars decked out with flowers and green leaves—bullocks drawing them with bells round their necks, and silver-plates on their heads—while every available post on the line of march was occupied by sweetmeat sellers, stalls of toys, and Surat and Poonah figures. They marched down to the sea-side, and every one tossed in their little temple, and then returned quietly home again. These exhibitions, observes Mr. Malcolm, not only present Doorga, but several images, often as large as life, very handsomely moulded, of wax, clay, or paper. The figure of Doorga which he thus describes, as seen at Calcutta, agrees with my own recollection of her at Bombay. "Under an ornamented canopy stands the goddess, stretching out her ten arms, each of which has a different occupation. One transfixes with a spear the giant Nahisha; others hold implements of war, flowers, sceptres, &c. Beneath her feet is a lion, tearing the said giant; and on each side are her sons, *Kartik* and *Ganesh*. The whole is borne on a frame or bier, requiring twenty bearers. The group is got up with much skill, and no little ornament, some of which is really tasteful and ornamental." In concluding his description of this festival, Mr. Malcolm observes, that "the men employed to cast the fabric into the river, no sooner got a little way from the shore in the boat, than they began to rifle the goddess of her muslins, plumes, and gilded ornaments, so that often nothing but a mere wreck was thrown overboard." I may remark that the figure was taken out at Bombay with all the drapery by those engaged to carry it when it arrived at the sea side, and only a trumpery frame work was placed on the head of a man who waded out and cast it from him into deep water. Upon enquiring the reason why the figure was not thrown in also, the person of whom I asked the question told me that the wax lady cost much money, and they should want her again for Pooja next year; a piece of economy with which I was much amused. There is seldom a month in which some of these festivals are not held, either by the Hindoos or Mohammedans; and so great is their attraction, that many of the public offices are closed for want of hands, and business is entirely suspended for the time. The Brahmins reap rich harvests during these feasts, and the hosts of religious mendicants, with their hair matted with cow dung, and their bodies smeared over with pigments, are set up once more with plenty of pocket-money, extorted from these simple and holiday-loving people. I have joined the gorgeous processions attending the betrothment of Hindoo children; a striking, though certainly a painful ceremony to witness, if we reflect, that the death of the boy, at this time only six or seven years old, will condemn his little innocent and unconscious bride to perpetual widowhood and low servitude. The children are brought together for the first time, and may never see one another again for years. Their parents often live some hundreds of miles apart; and when the time comes for the consummation of the marriage, the parties are perfect strangers to each other, and may, or may not live happily together. A cruel custom has left them no choice for themselves. Sordid avarice, high caste, and family aggrandizement, are but too often the motives of a Hindoo marriage, to the utter exclusion of the natural ties of a holy love. The Brahmin in blessing the pair, now perhaps twelve or fourteen years of age, scatters over them a handful of rice, emblematical of fruitfulness; his eye is then fixed on the trembling girl, as he directs her attention to the mystic fire burning between them, and suggestive of that fearful Suttee, which now, however, thanks to the humanity of England, and to the God who has taught her mercy, is abolished. Go, Hindoo girl, with the husband of thy youth, and if thou canst not now love him, may time endear him to thee: no sacrifice is now required of thee. Should it please Providence to make thee early a widow, thy life is still thy own, while Christian England protects thee. I have looked at all hours into the Indian temples, where crowds fell down and worshipped idols that bore but little resemblance to things on earth, or things under the earth; being in truth horrible caricatures of humanity; frightful monstrosities laved in rancid cocoa-nut oil, and bedaubed with red paint, over which a fair wreath of flowers withered in the tainted atmosphere. Round and round walked the worshippers, mumbling a vain repetition of some stated formula, till the eye was wearied by their motion, and the heart pained by the vanity of their superstition. They knew not God, and did but "grieve Him with their hill altars, and provoke him to displeasure with their images." In such visits I always met with kindness from those in charge of the temples. Many persons, as I was given to understand, had been rather rudely treated when inspecting these sanctuaries of idolatry; but from what I could learn, they had ridiculed all they saw, and treated the officers of these establishments with contempt and insolence. Can we be surprised at the reception they met with? Though I did not go beyond the porch as I should then have been obliged to uncover my feet according to the custom of the country, for leather shoes would have defiled the temple; yet I always removed my hat, as the ground upon which I stood appeared to me, in some sort, holy. Was it not, I thought, dedicated, however ignorantly, to the one great Father of all, who is indeed seen but darkly through his works by these my poor benighted fellow creatures? For them, as well as for myself, a dying Saviour had made an atonement on the cross, full, perfect, and finished; and does he not even now pity them, and would he not gladly gather them into his fold, even as he wept over the lost ones of Jerusalem? Some such feelings must arise in the mind of every reflecting man who enters these buildings.

Many of the English residents who live in confined bungalows, or have houses in the Fort, or other close buildings, obtain permission to erect tents and portable cottages during the hot season, on the open space of ground adjoining the esplanade. This situation is a delightful one to those who like a bustling and animated scene. A noble carriage-road runs through it, and of an evening, from five to seven o'clock, is crowded by an infinite variety of people of all classes and denominations, but more particularly by those who have been pent up all day in their offices. It is certainly the most fashionable resort on the island; every description of conveyance, from the two-hundred-guinea London Clarence, to the one-horse Shegram, and heavy rumbling native carriage and bullock hackery, finding its way hither, for an hour or two's display before dinner. The ground is a dead level for two miles, with Back Bay on one side and Bombay fort and harbour on the other; the road terminating in the new town. Few trees grow upon it, as they are supposed to obstruct the breeze and the view, which is excessively pretty. When the Commander-in-Chief has his tents pitched here, the attraction is doubly great, as a military band performs every evening opposite his compound; a treat not often enjoyed by the good people of Bombay, who have not a single public amusement, unless it be some stupid horse-races once a year; and a botanical garden, that nobody appears to take any interest in. Theatrical performances certainly were once attempted, but they met with but little encouragement in consequence of some characters of doubtful reputation appearing upon the boards. Many a half hour have I passed near this stand watching the natives, who delighted to throng round the musicians, exhibiting in their countenances various expressions of pleasure and surprise, as the rich notes floated sweetly upon the still evening air. Some were in fact "possessed beyond the muse's painting." The degraded and sensual Mohammedan, whose soul seldom soared beyond the regions of animal gratification, would pause here, as he passed by and caught the melodies of other lands; and the noisy occupants of the bullock-gharry would draw up their uncouth vehicle, and remain silent for the time. Groups of children sate around, but the passion for dancing, so universal in other countries, under the inspiration of music, was wanting among them; they were only attentive hearers like myself. On such occasions, thoughts that long had slept were revived, as the familiar notes recalled to memory days that had fled for ever; for

> "Like the gale that sighs along
> Beds of oriental flowers,
> Is the grateful breath of song,
> That once was heard in happier hours.
> Fill'd with balm the gale sighs on,
> Though the flowers have sunk in death;
> So when pleasure's dream is gone
> Its memory lives in music's breath."

Some of the Hindoos have a very high opinion of their own musical capabilities, and do not scruple to say, that the English are far behind them in this matter, and in horsemanship. The latter part of the assertion we may perhaps acknowledge. Many of the fine-weather houses erected on the esplanade are very pretty and ornamental; being principally constructed of bamboos, and having thatched roofs interwoven with cane-work. The gardens in front are separated by split bamboo paling, into which are tastefully trained flowering creepers and shrubs that have been grown elsewhere in tubs; while China jars and rustic seats combine to produce a pleasing effect. What was but a few weeks ago a long rambling piece of ground unoccupied excepting by a stray police-station, has thus been transformed into a busy little town. Officers on leave of absence from their regiments, or but newly arrived in the country, and other strangers, gladly avail themselves of the privilege granted them upon application, and pitch their camp tents here. Indian jugglers, *chumpri* or snake-charmers, and a variety of odd wandering characters peculiar to the East, add not a little to the amusements of this place. Here the young soldier mounts his new uniform for the first time in India, and gallops happily amidst the varied medley of rich and beautiful costumes. Near one of the gateways that lead into the Fort, may be seen a crowd of natives gathering together, who appear to be enjoying a hearty laugh at something in the centre of the group. We will take a peep at the object of this sport; an object, I regret to say, by no means uncommon here. One of those unfortunate specimens of our countrymen, a drunken English sailor, has been making a variety of ludicrous attempts to stand steady upon his own legs; but the demon spirit of cheap arrack tumbles him down again, and again the air is rent with the shouts and laughter of the ragged throng. He has no jacket on, for that has been stolen from him; and now he is threatening death and destruction to what he calls sons of niggers, and *petticoat* fellows who wont lend him a hand to help him up again upon his legs. He has been out to Dungaree, and, as a matter of course, has made himself most particularly tipsy amongst the Portuguese drinking-shops, in that famed locality, and has contrived to get so far towards his ship, having expended, perhaps, half his hard-earned wages during the last twenty-four hours, and completely verified the old saying, that "sailors earn their money like horses, and spend it too often like asses." Fortunately, however, for the credit of our country, the natives understand but little of what he says, though the words, "bad man," whispered among the better dressed, attracted to the spot, grates disagreeably upon our ears, and makes us feel not a little ashamed of our connection with this "son of the ocean." A policeman, in a yellow turban, blue gown, and red sash, finally drags him off to the *thanna*, till he sobers down again. The next morning, he returns to his ship in the harbour, robbed of his money and clothes, and, in all probability, dies in a day or two of brain-fever, from exposure to the sun. His friends at home are told that he fell a victim to the effects of the dreadfully unhealthy climate; for *the truth*, with respect to such matters, is seldom told; and in this manner are countries and places unjustly blamed; the habits of the deceased individual being quite overlooked or forgotten. *This is not in the least an exaggerated picture* of the way in which too many of our countrymen conduct themselves in the East. I have sketched it from the life. How often have I seen English sailors, overcome by the poisonous arrack and cheap spirits, which are so abundant, lying near the docks of Bombay, covered with bruises and flies, and fast asleep—such a sleep as the drunkard only knows,—blistering in a dreadful sun, the ridicule of what they call "*the heathen blacks.*" What an example is this! Surely we need not be surprised, that our missionaries make but few converts.

Tents may be purchased or hired from the manufacturers. Their charges vary from ten to twenty rupees a month, according to size and quality. It is surprising to see how quickly they will pitch you a large marquee. Stables, cooking-rooms, bath-rooms, &c., are all made neatly of the same material, and a great deal of taste is often displayed in their construction. It is some time before you become reconciled to this mode of living; for you cannot retire at night with that comfortable feeling of security that a stone-built house gives. One of the great disadvantages attending tent-living is, the annoyance which you suffer from mosquitoes, which, on some evenings, literally swarm around your rooms. These pests of the tropics delight in fastening themselves to the lining of the canvas, in the daytime, where they remain quiet and unobserved; but as soon as the evening shades prevail, and your lamps are lit at night, and you are comfortably settled with your book, the light attracts them at once, and each one sounds his well-known but dreadful note of war in your ears. That peculiar states of the weather have the effect of driving all the mosquitoes within doors, there can be little doubt; for I have observed that, on some evenings, your rooms are quite free from them, while on others, the nuisance is so great as to compel you to open all the flies and tapework windows, and to have them punkahed out by your servants.—From the low and swampy character of Bombay, so favourable to the propagation of these insects, we are not surprised at being told, upon landing in this island, that there are two luxuries you are never to expect to enjoy here—good water, and a quiet night's repose. So gently do the mosquitoes alight upon an exposed part, that you are never conscious of it, until they have insinuated their minute proboscis into an open pore, and laid the foundation of an hour or two's misery. A hungry mosquitoe will feast upon you, if undisturbed, for about twenty minutes. He generally, when he has the choice, selects a vein that is thinly covered with cuticle; but, when suffering from a long fast, he is not so particular, but bores down at a venture, until he reaches the life-stream; and, when satisfied, you are astonished to see the great change that has taken place in his appearance. The tiny body has become swollen as round as that of a spider; and he flies heavily away to some secluded corner, until the pangs of hunger again assail him. In this state he is a very tempting morsel to our friend the room-lizard. The wound, if not irritated, presents nothing to the eye but a small circular red patch, about the size of half a split pea; but if excited by friction, it rises into a hard little tumour, and, in some cases, will even run into a tedious sore. When the eyelids are attacked, which is not unusual during sleep, temporary blindness is not an uncommon result. It is curious the natives are seldom attacked by these insects. I was not a little interested in the subject, and made many inquiries to ascertain the truth of it; but whether it is their dark-coloured skin, or the oil that some of them use upon their persons, I believe that they are in a great measure protected from their attacks. A fresh arrival in the country claims their especial attention; and I have often pitied the tortures that some endure from these insect-enemies. When reading or writing, I was always obliged to wear gloves; and though they made the hands awfully hot, yet, of the two evils, the heat is the least. Blood is not the natural food of these insects, though they are so skilful in extracting it; marshy wooded lands, the banks of rivers, and old reservoirs, breed millions of mosquitoes, that can seldom have an opportunity of tasting blood. The common plumed gnat of England (Tipula plumicornis), is a small variety of this widely distributed insect. It may appear strange, that even in Lapland the inhabitants are so incommoded with swarms of gnats, that the poor people scarcely dare go abroad, without smearing their faces with a mixture of tar and cream, to protect them from their bites. Linnæus has thought, that, independently of their supplying nutritious food to innumerable birds and fish, mosquitoes and other winged pests are beneficial to the cattle which they attack, by inducing them to take exercise, and so preventing the ill effects of indolence and repletion in warm climates, where food is generally so plentiful, as to require but little searching after. Be this as it may, it is certain, that many an apparent evil in nature has been wisely ordained by the Almighty, for the universal good of all his creatures, though perhaps to the inconvenience of man.

There is a shelving bank that slopes down from the esplanade to the sea-shore, and here, of an evening, numbers of the poor natives assemble to pray at stated hours. I was often struck with the earnestness of their devotions, and became familiar with the faces of many who were most regular in their attendance.—One was an Arabian Jew; but why he came here to pray, I never could learn. Another was a very aged, tottering old man, with a beard of silvery whiteness, and a back bowed beneath the weight of years. His prayers were long and fervent; and it was impossible to look on him without feeling, that that man was "in audience with the Deity." With eyes raised upwards, as if endeavouring to penetrate the dark blue canopy overhead, his thoughts seemed fixed on something far removed beyond the grovelling things of earth. Could this man, I thought, be a blind idolator? Not far from him stood a tall Parsee, a man I knew to be engaged all day in business in the Fort; yet his worldly cares never appeared to interfere with his religious duties. At his feet lay his high card-board turban, for he stood uncovered during this solemn hour. Prayer after prayer was repeated by this earnest disciple of Zoroaster; and how often was the poor body prostrated and humbled to the very dust, as the little book from which he read his prayers, brought to his remembrance sins of which he had been guilty, or a feeling of his own unworthiness flashed across his mind! His favourite hour was when the sun was sinking to his rest; and as, from the bank, he obtained a view of the glorious departing orb as it dipt beneath the far horizon, and tinged the purple waters with a stream of refulgent light, again and again did the poor fire-worshipper throw himself forward upon the earth; again and again did he press his forehead as if in agony, and with arms stretched out towards the sinking luminary, again and again did he supplicate it to convey his sorrows and his repentance to the throne of Him whom he knew not how to approach in any other way. I could not but think, that this poor ignorant idolater was using to better purpose his one talent, the little light that had dawned upon his dark mind, than many Christians use the full blaze of gospel day.

Within a few yards of this interesting scene rolled the carriages of the wealthy children of England—of those who, like myself, had received ten talents.

Had they become familiar with, or indifferent to, the condition of these poor, deluded worshippers? or, was there nothing that they could do individually to assist the laborious efforts of the few missionaries who had been sent out to proclaim Christ crucified, in this land of pagan darkness? or, was it indeed true, that many had rather retarded than advanced that righteous cause in India, by their own bad example and lax morality? Let us hope, that it was not altogether thus; yet it is true, that we have made but slow progress in the great work of evangelizing India, during the nearly two hundred years that have elapsed since the British flag first floated over the battlements of Surat. Were it not for the massive tower of the Cathedral, and the tapering spire of the Scotch Church, a stranger would at times almost doubt whether Christianity had ever been introduced at Bombay; where thousands yet fall down to worship their graven images. How is it, we may ask, that we can always find money to protect the country with our armies, to raise magnificent palaces for our governors, to fortify our possessions, to sustain an Indian navy, to construct public roads and canals, to unite our towns and cities by projected railways, to contribute £6000 a year to support the brutal rites and atrocious barbarities connected with the blood-thirsty temple of Juggernaut, and yet say, that we cannot afford to send out a few more missionaries, in return for the enormous sums drawn from our Indian possessions?

> "Can these things be,
> And overcome us, like a summer's dream,
> Without our special wonder?"

Four more bishops are at length to be sent out, in order to lighten the onerous duties of those already appointed. This is a gratifying movement in the right direction. Conscience is beginning to accuse us of our guilty neglect of India. But we want more field-labourers; men who will go out into her highways and byways—into her jungle-villages and her mountain-fastnesses—into those wild and secluded districts, where the feet of him who bringeth good tidings of great joy have never yet brushed away the dews of the morning.

It is nearly thirty-six years since Dr. Middleton was appointed first Bishop of Calcutta, with episcopal authority over the *whole* of *British India*. He was a man of great piety and learning, and founded "Bishop's College." He was succeeded by the accomplished Reginald Heber, who carried out many of his predecessor's good designs, but who was removed by an early death from the sphere of his usefulness. It has been observed, that these two first appointments were most happily made, and that lawn has seldom been worn by better men. Since then, Bombay, Madras, and Agra, have been made separate bishoprics; but even with this addition to the ecclesiastical staff, it was found quite impossible to keep pace with the growing wants of so large a country. The Presidency of Bombay alone contains a large extent of Aurungabad, Candeish, and Guzerat; and the number of souls under the British government in India has been computed at 80,000,000. The establishment of public schools in many of our large towns, where all the useful branches of a religious and sound English education are taught to the native scholars, has already worked wonders at the presidencies. A writer in the Quarterly Review, in dwelling upon this all-important subject, has remarked that "a general knowledge of history or geography will at once disperse that cloud of more than Egyptian darkness, which for so many ages had confined their view. . . . When they cease to consider Mount Meru as twenty thousand miles high, and the world as a flower, of which India is the cup, and other countries the leaves, their minds may become more open to rational views on the subject of religion."

CHAPTER VIII.

" The moon, refulgent lamp of night,
O'er heaven's clear azure spreads her sacred light,
When not a breath disturbs the deep serene,
And not a cloud o'ercasts the solemn scene.
Around her throne the vivid planets roll,
And stars unnumbered gild the glowing pole;
O'er the dark trees a yellower verdure shed,
And tip with silver every mountain's head."

Departure of day. Rapid advance of night. Indian nights peculiar. Deserted roads. Sepoy guards and flight of the begging crowds. Mosques The cunning snake charmer. Mohammedan devotee. A poor Sudra. Large edible bat and beetles. The music of Nature. Elater Noctilucus. Infinity of living creatures. Funeral pyres. Back bay. Vultures. Covering a body. Burning it. Friends of departed. Children's indifference to the dead. Shore strewed with human bones. Hindoos on death. Government proclamations. Nizam of Hyderabad. Do the Brahmins encourage self-immolation ? Dangers of the coast. Fate of the Donna Pascoa. Romantic story of Colabah. English residences. Parsee property. The nest of the tailor warbler. Barracks and soldiers. Predisposing causes to cholera. Contagion. Sick bungalows. English chapel and old tombs. Sea-shells and cowries. Land-crabs, their habits and haunts, &c., &c.

THE great orb of day has rolled down into the far west, but its lingering glory is still reflected everywhere around us. We can trace it gilding the tops of the mosques and spires, and burnishing the green leaves of the cocoa-nut palms, as they move gently in the evening breeze. We can track it over the wide expanse of waters, as it brings out in fine relief a lone sail, homeward bound; we can see it in the rich purple haze that floats over all things. If we turn our eyes towards the east, we are surprised to see how rapidly night is advancing upon us, and how speedily the lofty mountains and the towering peak, known as the "Queen of Mahratta's needle," are becoming veiled from our view. Lights begin to glimmer here and there upon the coast, and the darkened sky over the horizon is illumined for hours after sunset, by flashes from clouds charged with the electric fluid. The transition from day to night, in those parts of India that are situated between the tropics, being very sudden, we, here, know very little of that lingering of the sun's reflected rays, which constitutes the twilight of northern climes. The heavens are for a brief space tinged with the hues of all glorious things, unutterably, indescribably beautiful, and then the brilliant picture fades away.

We must now again turn our attention to earth, and take, during these quiet hours, a passing glance at the scenes around us; for an Indian night has a character of its own. The noise and bustle of the busy day are over; the crowded esplanade is all but deserted; the prayerful Parsee has quitted the sea-shore; the last carriage, with its pale and languid occupants, has passed through the gateway that leads into the Fort;

the evening tattoo has been rolled at the barracks; the tired sentinel has been relieved from his post of duty; and the heavy tramp of the sepoy guard, as he paces slowly up and down before the low sallyport, halting occasionally to challenge the stray rambler with the accustomed interrogatory, *quon-hie?* (Who goes there?) is just heard to fall upon the dull ear of night. If we look across the battlements, we see rows of bright lamps burning in some of the high houses, which are occupied by English families, and of which the inhabitants have now thrown wide open the large Venetian shutters, in order to give free admittance to the night air; and we may even detect from our position upon the esplanade, the incessant movements of room-punkahs, and the restlessness of those who are pacing to and fro, in consequence of the excessive heat. The idle, begging crowds, that had for hours haunted the entrances to the neighbouring mosques, have now dispersed for the night; and the great Hindoo temple dedicated to *Momba Devi*, has echoed back the last prayers of its idolatrous worshippers. The wretched cripple, who, helpless as an infant, had lain all day upon its steps, covered with sores like a second Lazarus, has been carried home on a stretcher by his friends, to lose a few hours in sleep, but to open his eyes on the morrow, to another day of misery. The cunning snake-charmer has twisted the fangless cobra-di-capello round his neck; has rolled up his painted sticks and brass balls; has made his final salaam to the gaping multitude, and has started off to his native village, to enjoy the profits of his day's deception, and to laugh in secret at the credulity of mankind. The Mohammedan devotee creeps into his mat-covered hut, and has strangely found again the use of the withered arm, which, during the whole past day, standing by the side of the public footpath, he has held up as an immovable member; and now counts over the many *pice* that the hand of charity has compassionately bestowed upon him, in accordance with the Prophet's precepts. He has made a flourishing trade of his pretended religion, and lives upon the labour of the industrious few. India is heavily taxed by these impostors, and throughout its length and breadth, groans under their numbers. There is a poor Sudra, a hard-working man, wending his way homeward, tired and weary, over the hot dusty road. His feverish day has been passed in one of those grim old buildings near the dock-yard, in packing raw cotton into bales for exportation, to be unpacked by his fellow-labourers in Manchester and elsewhere. But how superior is their lot to his; they have no suffocating heat, in which to toil; to their name there is attached no debasing caste, which will prevent—shall I say for ever?—the poor Indian labourer from rising in the social scale of civilization. Life, to him, is but a season of toil and insult, of which in eternity he expects but the renewal; for, within the gates of Paradise he, as he is taught to believe, can never enter; but must still labour outside, for the benefit and luxury of the faithful chosen ones. He knows not, that the Great Proprietor has given a free invitation to *all* who will come unto him with a humble and a contrite spirit. His day has been a day of suffering, but it is over now; and with the few *annas* secreted in the folds of his ragged turban, he trudges homeward, content, if not grateful, to partake of a frugal repast of rice and plantains; and after having enjoyed his hookah, and a bath, and a half hour's communion with the red idol in the centre of his dwelling, he will sleep well by the side of his simple family, away among the cocoa-nut plantations, which are so dimly and indistinctly seen from the spot on which we stand. The large edible bat startles us in our meditations, as he hovers between us and the bright stars, like a blot upon the face of the heavens. How swiftly does he sail along upon his leathern wings, cleaving the air, unheard by us; soft and noiseless! His home is in the ruined temples of Salsette and Elephanta. Night has tempted him abroad; and his keen eyes detect the dancing insects that, (attracted by the lights within,) hum in myriads between the rows of white tents scattered near the shore. The withered grass at our feet appears to be filled with life. Large beetles are issuing from the sun-cracks in the earth, and are rattling their hard cases against the dry stubble as they rise heavily into the cool air, and add their buzzing voices to the music of the night. The firefly (Elater noctilucus) hastens to join the glowing circles that play joyously under the old jack-trees, near the sanitarium; now lighting up the cups of fresh-blown flowers, now ranging over the still tanks where the spotted frog croaks undisturbed upon the buoyant leaves. Crickets weary the ear with their eternal chirping; and the timid musk-weasel utters its piercing cry, as we stumble over it in our path. Every thing around us teems with life; and ere daylight has bid farewell to earth, night sends forth her mighty hosts to re-people the world. Vain would be the attempt of man to try even to enumerate, much more to classify, the infinity of creatures, great and small, that between sunset and sunrise, move abroad on the earth, or fan the light air with their wings. The mind becomes confused by the mere idea of such an undertaking.

There is one spectacle which particularly attracts our attention, and which is perhaps more worthy of our notice than the objects upon which I have so hurriedly touched. It is the blazing upon the shores of Back Bay, of the funeral pyres, which, in the still hours of evening, often illuminate the heavens, and scare the wild sea-birds as they return to their place of roosting among the high cliffs on Malabar point.

My first visit to this Hindoo Golgotha is still fresh upon my memory; for it left a strong impression not easily to be effaced. Five or six of these pyres had been erected at the head of the bay; a district that has, I believe, for ages been set apart for the purpose of burning the bodies of the dead. One evening, soon after my arrival in the island, curiosity tempted me to ride out in that direction, in order to see these supposed beacons, which I had fancied were lit to guide the fishing-boats home at night. My surprise was great upon going up to one of them, to see the legs of a dead Hindoo protruding from between the logs of timber that were, ere long, to consume the body. The pyre was about five feet high, and having been clumsily built, it had, in consequence, given way at one end; a circumstance which had not escaped the prying eyes of some huge fulvous vultures, which were screaming overhead, and making sundry dives downwards, towards this attractive spot, and which did not appear in the least to thank me for disturbing them. About fifty yards from this pyre was another, on which was stretched the body of either a young man or a female, which some attendants, with a carelessness of manner which showed little regard for the deceased, were busily covering with small fagots about a foot in length, which they pitched on to the pile from a bullock-cart near at hand. After a sufficient quantity of wood had been piled up, a torch was applied to some inflammable material at the base, and within an hour afterwards the whole was one mass of fierce fire. There did not appear to be any form or religious ceremony whatever; nor was there any weeping or lamentation, or other outward sign of grief, from those who stood around, three or four of whom I fancied were relatives; but "the heart may break without a tear," and the sorrows of some of these by-standers might be deep and lasting, though I could not detect them. There they stood silent; and apparently unmoved, watching the angry flames as they devoured the mortal body of one who had now put on immortality! As soon as they were satisfied that the wood was well ignited, they all walked away together, towards a plantation, where stands a ruined temple, under cover of which the whole party was lost to my view, with the exception of one woman, who again paused for a moment as if to take a last farewell. I would have given much could I have known her real feelings, and what was passing in her mind. Lower down upon the shore were a company of children playing round the dying embers of a funeral pyre, just as if it had been a fifth of November bonfire; but they from their infancy, had been familiar with these scenes of death; and they had, for them, no terror. The neighbourhood of this place of burning was strewed with human bones, some, partly calcined, others, quite perfect, and white as the driven snow, from having been tossed about by the waves at high water, and left to bleach in the sun. The perfect bones were those of children, who are buried here in the sands; and whose bones are generally disinterred by the first springs that flow up to them; the natives seldom take the trouble to bury them deep enough to secure them against such casualties.

The Hindoo custom of burning their adult dead

is a very ancient one; and it is thought to have had its origin in the popular superstition current among them, that, after the body has been destroyed by fire, no evil being can have any further power over the emancipated spirit. The Hindoos believe, that should this religious duty be omitted through neglect, the surviving friends of the departed, will, in all probability, have their happiness disturbed by frequent visits from some unclean migratory soul, which in that case is supposed to make a point of taking immediate possession of the unburned and vacant tenement. It has been stated, that during the late wars in India the anxiety of the native soldiers to burn their slain brethren-in-arms, was so great, that they would often run the utmost risk of being taken prisoners, in their endeavours to procure wood for the purpose. This feeling is happily all that is now left to preserve the memory of the dreadful Suttee, which, by the persevering efforts and determined conduct of its Anglo-Indian rulers, is now all but absolutely abolished throughout our Indian empire. From the time of Warren Hastings down to the governorship of Lord Hardinge, each successive governor-general of our Indian possessions has done something towards this good work; and though it has been one of time and caution, acts of prohibition have been yearly made more stringent, as previous laws proved insufficient to meet the evil; and many native princes have now voluntarily come forward to aid our present government in carrying out its good intentions.

Proclamations have recently been issued by the Bengal government, stating, that no fewer than twenty-three princes and chiefs have been induced to abolish the horrible custom, and with it, female infanticide, throughout their dominions. The Sikh ruler of Jamoo has, unsolicited, followed their noble example; and the Nizam of Hyderabad has issued a mandate to the same effect. Truly in all this there is matter of rejoicing. If England had done nothing more than this for the good of her Indian possessions, she would have accomplished a great work; seeing that it was computed, that, at one time, from forty to fifty thousand females annually sacrificed themselves to the flames, under the foolish and vain idea that by so doing, they would be permitted to enjoy Paradise with their husbands for threescore and fifty lacks of years, or about thirty million and fifty thousand years. Such, I believe, were the promises held out to them by their priests; though it has been denied, that the Brahmins encouraged them in their self-immolation.

Back Bay, to all appearance a beautiful and well-sheltered roadstead, is unfit, as a place of anchorage, for shipping of any burthen; the bottom of it being covered with very dangerous rocks, which run out in a sort of reef into the open sea. Occasionally this bay has been the scene of some awful wrecks, in consequence of having been mistaken in the night for Bombay harbour; the two bays being separated only by a narrow strip of land, known to mariners as "Old

Woman's Island," or Colabah. The *Donna Pascoa*, and the *Lord William Bentinck*, two noble vessels, were wrecked here, a short time before my arrival. The south-west monsoon was raging at the time, when one of them ran upon the reef of rocks; and, expecting to go to pieces every moment, they burnt a light in her bow, and sent up rockets, in the hope of gaining some assistance from those on shore. While in this distressing position, the *Lord William Bentinck* was making for Bombay harbour; and seeing this light burning on board the ship ashore, and another in the light-house not far off, her captain became confused, and altered her course a little, and, in consequence, struck upon a bar at the entrance of the real harbour. The scene next morning was described to me as an awful one; but many of the passengers were saved. I had the pleasure of seeing a poor little girl, who had been washed out of the arms of her mother, and was driven ashore, *alive*, upon the breast of a heaving wave.

Colabah can now scarcely be called an island, as a splendid valade, built at a great expense, for the accommodation of the public, unites it, at its most southern point with Bombay. A melancholy and romantic story is still told of Colabah. Before Bombay was united to Colabah by the valade alluded to, it was often impossible, though the distance was very trifling, to go from one island to the other without a boat; for, during the rise of the tide, the sea rushed through this little strait with great force and rapidity, although at low water a person might have walked across, I believe, without wetting his feet. A young girl, of the Mohammedan faith, was on her road to pay a visit to some natives, who resided in Colabah; and having arrived in her *bullock-gharry*, just when the tide was rising in this place, she thought, that as the water was not deep, she might cross without danger, and ordered her *syce*, or driver, to urge the timid bullocks across the stream. He did so; but before they had proceeded many yards, the animals became restive and obstinate, and refused to go one way or another; the wheels became entangled among the rough stones; the *gharry* was upset, and the poor girl, being thrown into the rapidly increasing current, was swept out into Back Bay. This scene was witnessed, most fortunately, from the Colabah side, by an Englishman, who had up to this moment been a passive spectator. In an instant his coat was off, and he was breasting the foaming tide after the drowning girl; whom, at the risk of his own life, he succeeded in bringing safely to the shore. He accompanied her home to Bombay, where he received the thanks and benediction of her parents. Strange to say, but not more strange than true, an attachment sprang up between the young Englishman and the Hindoo lady whom he had rescued from a watery grave; and many were said to be the private meetings that took place between the two lovers—unknown, of course, to the unsuspecting parents. At length, the Englishman, though he well knew that his religion would be an insuperable objection, determined to solicit, from her father, the Mohammedan girl's hand in marriage. He did so, and the haughty man of high caste at once indignantly spurned his proposals. He acknowledged that he loved the fair Englishman, but he never could be one of his *people;* so he bade him depart in peace. The sequel was very sad. The Hindoo maiden disappeared. Rumours were current, in Bombay, that she had been privately murdered by her enraged relatives; but I do not suppose it was ever certainly known what became of her, though the matter was said to have been investigated by those in authority. One of rumour's hundred reports at length reached the ears of our poor countryman, who had "loved not wisely, but too well;" the shock was too great to bear; he died suddenly, the victim of a broken heart. The whole family of the maiden left the island, in consequence of the suspicion attached to them; and so ended this strange eventful history. After hearing this story, I seldom passed over the valade, without thinking of the poor drowning girl, and of my own brother, who had nearly lost his life in the same way, before this dangerous place had been made secure to travellers in all states of the tide.

The small promontory of Colabah is naturally connected with Bombay by a mass of whinstone rocks, which, however, do not rise above the surface of the waters. It runs out for about two miles into the sea, in rather a south-westerly direction, and forms a sort of tongue between Bombay harbour and Back Bay.

On its extreme point is erected a light-house, which rises one hundred and fifty feet above the level of the ocean, and may be seen, in clear weather, at the distance of seven or eight leagues from the coast. It is considered a healthy place of residence, being freely exposed to the sea-breeze; and its beauty is greatly enhanced by the charming view which it commands on all sides. In consequence of these advantages, it is crowded by English, Parsee, and Portuguese bungalows; which are all detached residences, surrounded by luxuriant gardens, redolent of sweet flowers. The walks are very cool, being well shaded from the sun; and there is a delightful drive through the island to the battery, which is built near the light-house. The property on this island belongs, principally, like much of the property in Bombay, to Parsees; and a great number of the houses are rented solely by English merchants, who rejoice to live there; being able to see, from their terraces, every vessel that enters the harbour, and to catch the first glimpse of the overland mail, the monthly bearer of joy or sorrow, as she steams up to her anchorage off the Apollo bunda, and announces her arrival by the cannon's mouth. The boundary-hedges are enriched by a charming creeping plant, which bears a scarlet, and sometimes a rich mazarine-blue pea-flower. When in full bloom, these plants add greatly to the beauty of the compounds. The "morning's glory," a majestic description of convolvulus, wraps itself, after the conclusion of the rainy season, round the palms, and perfectly enchants you by its exquisite colours, as its blossoms swing from the crowned top. This island, like Bombay and many others in its neighbourhood, was originally covered with dense forests of the cocoa-palm and other trees, but they have been cleared away in many places, to make room for public buildings, roads, &c.

In one of the delicious compounds of Colabah, I had an opportunity of examining, for the first time, the nest of the "tailor-warbler." A pair of these interesting little birds had selected the large leaf of a plant growing in a stand close to the porch of a bungalow, and having curiously drawn the edges of the leaf, three or four inches above the foot-stalk, together, had secured them effectually in that position, by sewing them with some fine vegetable fibre; thus forming a cone, in which they had deposited their nest, which was a beautiful specimen of bird-architecture, composed chiefly of cotton wool, and of other soft downy materials, carefully interwoven together. The nest was not entirely concealed, for a portion of its rim was so contrived as to hang over the side, and thus giving additional support to the fabric when occupied. The leaf, though thus confined, appeared to be healthy; for instinct had taught its little tenants not to wound with their bills, when sewing it, the large arteries which nourished it. These little birds were carefully protected by the lady of the house, who took a great interest in their welfare; and the servant had strict orders to avoid, as much as possible, disturbing the female, particularly during the process of incubation. They succeeded, to the joy of every one, and particularly myself, in bringing forth a young family; but with the ill fortune of many pets of this description, that have sought the protection of man, they did not escape the prying eyes of a large Persian cat, which belonged to some old bachelor near. One morning a terrible chirping and fluttering was heard, and my friend suspecting the cause, ran into the garden. Alas! she was too late! Puss had scampered off across the grounds with one of the young birds in her mouth; the leaf was broken, and the remaining birds dead from the fall. The nest and leaf were dried, and carefully preserved, as furnishing a curiosity for friends at home.

Colabah has been selected as the site for a lunatic asylum, and for barracks for the accommodation of troops landing from England; chiefly, because the soldiers are here a good deal out of the way of temptation, as drinking cannot be followed up in this small island, with the facilities which are afforded them in the Fort and new town. Arrack and other spirits are so cheap in India, that a man who has a fancy for drinking, upon coming out to this country is pretty certain to fall a victim to cholera, or to some of the other diseases peculiar to the East; and in fact the number of deaths that, resulting from this vice alone, thin our European regiments, is very great, I am tempted here to make an extract from a report on this subject, addressed by Alexander Thom, Esq., surgeon in her Majesty's 86th regiment, to the Army Medical Board in London.

After tracing some of the predisposing causes to the fearful mortality that attended this regiment, which landed in Bombay during the wet season, July, 1842, and showing that forced marches, harassing duty, encamping in tents, and vicissitudes of temperature, had, all and each, their share in the work of death, Mr. Thom proceeds as follows :—"There is another undeniable, and *almost incalculable predisposing cause* of disease, alike common in the 86th and other European corps, in this and in other garrisons in India; viz., the use of raw and ardent spirits. While I admit the extent of this evil, I do not mean to say that it was greater in the 86th than in any other corps. I have taken the trouble to possess myself of information in figures on this subject, which satisfies me, that what I state is exactly correct. The soldiers were allowed to obtain four drams or 'tots' of arrack, daily, the amount of which, when put together, is about half a common bottle. If a man does not exceed this, he thinks himself temperate, and is considered so in his regiment. Many, of course, do not avail themselves of this indulgence, but there are few who do not take two drams daily. Day by day this practice is followed by too many men, *and permitted.*"

These men, as we find from the Report from which I have made an extract, were the greatest sufferers from cholera, in this and other regiments, to which Mr. Thom alludes; though he says, that he does not mean to infer that inebriety was in *every* case visited by this scourge of the East. The soldiers suffered most; their wives next; the children and officers still less; while *ladies* had a total exemption from this fearful malady. Had it been, as he observes, contagious, all were equally liable to its attacks; in fact, scarcely an officer's compound entirely escaped it; yet, out of forty-two ladies living in the cantonment at Kurrachee, only one had a slight and doubtful attack of cholera, and not one died. This he attributes to temperance; to the absence of fatigue and night marches; and to living in cool and well-ventilated bungalows; seeing that these ladies were subject, in common with the soldiers, to the same atmospheric changes; and that it was certainly not their sex which protected them, as the soldiers' wives suffered severely.

The East India Company have erected, on Colabah, comfortable buildings, for the benefit of invalid officers who may require sea air or sea bathing. These buildings are called the "sick bungalows," and are enclosed in a spacious compound. Close to the principal entrance is a jack-tree, much decayed, and supposed to be one of the oldest trees now standing on any of these islands. About half a mile to the south of the sick bungalow, and adjoining the parade-ground, is a neat little thatched chapel, where the English service is performed; but all who wish to avail themselves of it must bring their own chairs, as it does not contain any seats. I went two or three times, and heard pleasing discourses from the Rev. Mr. Pigot, the gentleman who usually officiates there. A few old Mohammedan tombs still rear their domed roofs among the cocoa-nut trees; and some very ancient Portuguese houses, crumbling into ruins, recall to memory the wealthy merchants who once occupied these islands, and the heavily-laden Spanish galleons that were wont to sail from these shores, to enrich the nobles of Spain, or to gild the palaces of the Venetians. The sea-shore here was a favourite morning ramble of mine; and the collecting of the variety of beautiful shells, which here abound, afforded me amusement and instruction. The shells are literally thrown up in heaps by the tide; though the large leopard-cowry was the only one of any size which I met here. There were numbers of the acorn, spine, variegated cockle, spiral, snail, and bivalve shells; madripores, scipia or cuttle-fish bones, pumice-stone, and many interesting marine productions, that enabled me to fill a good-sized box in a few days. The small cowries are sought after here by the natives; for in many parts of India they still pass current for money; and to say a thing is not worth a cowrie, is a common bazaar expression. Cowries vary in value in different places. At Calcutta—

4 cowries are equal to	1 gunda.
20 gundas - -	1 pon.
32 pons - -	1 current rupee, or 2560 cowries.

A curious species of land-crab infested the shores of Colabah. I fancy these crabs must have been the *occypodes*, or swift-footed crab, of the naturalist; if not, they well deserved the name. Hundreds might be seen at a time, in the morning and evening, hunting about for any stray food that the sea or the fishermen might have left. When disturbed, they ran with incredible swiftness, holding high above their bodies two extended claws, which they would knock together with a singular sound, as if to intimidate their enemies. As they ran into holes which they had formed in the bank, that gently shelved down to the shore, I used sometimes to perplex them, by placing a stone over the entrance of their holes, and giving chace to the excluded owner. Upon finding that his own door was closed against him, he would remain stationary for a second or two, as if determining what to do next; then he would start off, and bolt down the first hole in his road. If it chanced to be already occupied, the lawful tenant and the intruder soon re-appeared upon the surface, and a fierce fight ensued. The body of these curious and amusing crabs, which are of a light brown colour, and much about the same size, is about an inch long, and almost spherical in shape. They have, beside their claws, four delicate long legs on each side, each armed with a sort of hook. The claws are small and long, and capable of grasping and carrying firmly a very large substance. The eyes are protuberant and horny, like those of the common salt-water crab. I am inclined to think, that these crabs are the same which Bishop Heber met with near Poonah, and which are thus described by him :—"The plain of Poonah is very bare of trees; and though there are some gardens immediately around the city, yet as both these and the city itself is in a small hollow on the banks of the river Moolah, they are not sufficiently conspicuous to interrupt the general character of nakedness in the picture, any more than the few young trees and ornamental shrubs with which the bungalows of the cantonment are intermingled. The principal and most pleasing feature is a small insulated hill immediately over the town, with the temple of the goddess Parvati on its summit, and a large tank (which, when I saw it, was nearly dry,) at its base. All the grass-land round this tank, and generally through the Deccan, swarms with a small land-crab, which burrows in the ground, and runs with considerable swiftness, even when encumbered with a bundle of food almost as big as itself. This food is grass, or the green stalks of rice; and it is amusing to see them sitting as it were upright, to cut their hay with their sharp pincers, and then waddling off with the sheaf to their holes, as quickly as their sidelong pace will carry them." As it has been commonly supposed that all land-crabs retired at certain seasons of the year to the sea-side to deposit their eggs in salt-water, Mr. Broderip has made an interesting observation respecting the land-crabs spoken of by Bishop Heber. In the fourth volume of the Zoological Journal, he says, that "when we call to mind the position of Poonah, and read of the neighbouring river and tank, we may feel inclined to ask whether the river or the tank might not be the scene of ovipositing;" and, he adds, that "it is not improbable that there may be a race of land-crabs appropriated to continental, or even insular situations out of reach of the ocean, and that fresh water may be as necessary to their re-production as sea-water is to the land-crabs of the West Indies. Such a supposition," he thinks, "is in unison with the bountiful provisions of Nature for the general diffusion of animal life."

Bidding adieu to the land-crabs and to Colabah, we will now turn our attention to some of the natives, who, in the way of their respective occupations, minister so largely to an Englishman's comfort and happiness in India; and whose useful services may be said to be indispensable in every bungalow.

CHAPTER IX.

"I have known cases in which a kind-hearted woman would have esteemed herself robbed of a privilege, if her lover had asked any other person than herself so much as to mend his glove, yet is it not impossible for the same woman two years after marriage, to say—'my sister, or my cousin, will do that for you. I am too busy now.'"

MRS. ELLIS,—"WOMEN OF ENGLAND."

Establishment of a wealthy merchant. Three classes of servants. Ladies' maids and Ayehs. Affection of Indian nurses, their love for your children. Sketch of a Dobie or washer-man. How to get up linen. Advice to new arrivals. Sketch of the Bheestie, or water-bearer. The grunt at your bed room door. The Delhi brooch. Temptations to be avoided. Sketch of the Dergie or plain sewing-man. His beautiful work. English ladies and poor husbands. A box on the ear for stupidity. Indian butter. An old favourite. Sketch of Meeta and Metrane sweepers. Poor despised people. Chandalas forbidden to reside in towns. Their calling. Grave-diggers and executioners. The First visitor at your Bungalow. Troubles with superstitious servants. The Molly or gardener. The Garry-Wallah and his horses. Indian Jewellers. Their tools and workmanship. Wealth and talents. How to make a gold chain. Danger of fraud, &c., &c.

MAN is every where a dependent creature, constantly looking to others for support and assistance; and I scarcely know of any country where he feels this dependence more than in India. In the case of an Englishman, the climate alone is sufficient to produce this effect. The domestic establishment of a wealthy merchant is not thought to be complete unless he have eighteen or twenty paid servants in his employ. This display of slaves, as they were absurdly called, (for a man cannot be a slave who is master of his own liberty, and properly remunerated for his services,) does not arise from any particular love of having a great show of these people in your pay, but simply from the circumstance that the individual services of each cannot be dispensed with. Nearly half your servants are kept entirely as palanquin-bearers, and men to look after your horses and carriages. The servants who reside on your premises may be divided into three distinct classes—Portuguese, Hindoos, and Mohammedans; in order that one man may be useful, when another's religion will not allow him to be so. Each has his separate work allotted to him; and with this understanding they get on very well together. Your Mohammedan servants will not clean your boots, because the brushes are made of the bristles of the hateful animal; your Hindoo servants will not touch a plate or dish that has been defiled by yourself, or by a Portuguese; and hence arises the necessity of having servants of different castes. It was the custom formerly,—perhaps as matter of fashion,—for a family going out to India to take with them a well-educated lady's-maid, who could fulfil all the duties belonging to her station, and also, when necessary, assist in the instruction of your children. This of course could only be accomplished by a wealthy family, and involved a serious outlay and responsibility. However, it was the fashion; and numbers of young females, often respectably connected, thus found their way out to India. If they were good looking, they seldom remained six months unmarried; and even those least favoured in outward attractions soon found a partner and a home amidst the hundreds of single old gentlemen, who wanted housekeepers rather than wives, to complete their happiness in their adopted country. The consequence of all this was, that English ladies got tired of trying experiments which proved so costly. *Ayehs* came into fashion, and *ladies'-maids* went out. Your Ayeh, or nurse, takes care of your children in the day, and sleeps in the same room with them at night. She is often a faithful creature, and remains with you for life. She loves, to distraction, your little ones; and they return it, by scarcely ever bearing to be out of her sight. Her affection becomes so strong, that she will often relinquish every tie that binds her to her native land, to follow you, and the objects of her unconquerable attachment. She teaches your children little Indian songs and tales; many of which are very beautiful, and it is marvellous how soon they pick up from her the language of the country, acting as they often do as little interpreters to their parents. The Ayeh spends all her spare money if not prevented, in buying little *missey* and *massa* Poonah and

Surat toys and sweetmeats. Her idle hours are passed in the manufacture of elephants, lions, and tigers, out of cloth, and stuffed with saw-dust or sandal-wood powder, as rewards to the children, for good behaviour. She can use her needle, but prefers sitting on the floor and teaching your eldest boy how to make a turban out of his father's red sash, or her own sarree. The Ayeh has often the entire care of the Anglo-Indian family where the mother has been taken away from among them. The one I have sketched here was so situated. She was an old woman, and had grown grey and wrinkled in her master's service. The little ones called her "mother," the elder children "Ayeh dear," for she had been a kind good nurse to all of them. "She is a fine character," said the widowed Dr. Y. to me one day, "and the only person I have about me that I can really trust." Many are the bitter tears often shed, when circumstances compel you to leave behind the poor Ayeh, who has nursed the rising family, now about to sail for England.

The *dobie*, or washerman, you may engage at so much a month, according to the number, or the wants of your family. He comes to your bungalow once a week, and brings with him his own servants to carry away the articles upon which he is to exercise his detergent art; you give him a list of them, which list your *musshall* reads over to him in Hindostanee; he marking it off in his own way, and you keeping another list yourself. If your family is a numerous one, there is a mountain-heap awaiting him at the end of the week; for the preservation of health demands, especially during the hot season, perpetual change of raiment. The *dobie* takes your belongings out about a mile into the country, where there are some large washing-tanks provided; and after having dipped them in a description of bleaching liquid, he and his men set to work to beat them on stones, till fully cleansed. After this process, they are passed through fresh water, and spread out to dry in the sun; a work which occupies but a few minutes, and which makes them snowy white. Of course this beating process, which is carried on for some time, soon destroys your garments; buttons fly about in all directions, and hooks and eyes are for ever separated. The articles are then taken home to be ironed, which is done by passing over them, in the usual manner, a square brass box, filled with heated stones and charcoal embers. Such things as require starching, or what ladies call "getting up," are dipped into a curious farinaceous compound, called *conjee*, and prepared from arrow-root and rice. Nor is the Indian *dobie* ignorant of the mysteries of stiffening lace, cambric, &c., only he never puts any blue into his preparations; water and everything else is a dead white; and, in consequence, everything on which he exercises his skill soon turns yellow, like the lace once thought so valuable. As the destruction of buttons, &c., is carried on, on a ruinous scale, *studs* are used in India wherever the substitution is practicable. They can be purchased from the native jewellers, finely executed in gold, silver, or Cambay pebbles. It is seldom that the *dobie* loses any of your apparel, for his eye soon becomes familiar with your private mark on them ; and until this is the case, you may expect to receive occasionally the property of others. His caste has the reputation of honesty; but, as a precautionary measure, the old Anglo-Indian strongly advises you always to have a month's pay in hand, in case of accident. I remember one, and I think only one instance of dishonesty on the part of this functionary; and it occurred in the house in which I resided, and which contained a number of boarders. Among other things, some very valuable French lace was carried off, and never recovered.—Information was quickly given to the police, but the man of suds had decamped from the island, taking away with him a large amount of property belonging to six other families. The loss to my landlord was about twenty pounds. There is manufactured in Bombay a particular kind of soap, which has the useful property of enabling you to use sea-water for cleansing purposes; and which consequently is much prized by sailors, who seldom fail to lay in a stock of it for their voyage home.

The *bheestie*, or *pawney-wallah*, supplies your bungalow every morning with fresh water. He brings it in the skin of a sheep sewed up, with one leg left for a spout; the whole being secured by a leathern cord slung over the left shoulder. He is a gentleman who stands upon very little ceremony with you, and hurries from one room to another, to fill the bath, chatties, and jugs, whether the apartments be occupied or not. His visits are paid *very* early in the morning, so that you may have the water as cool as possible; and he troubles himself not at all as to whether you are in bed or out of it—married or single. In he rushes, dripping wet, and leaving behind him a stream of the precious fluid; for his skins are always bad ones, and out gushes the water into your vessels, and away he hurries to the next room. Sometimes, indeed, you meet with a polite *pawney wallah;* one who will give a *grunt* outside your door, as a sort of warning to you to be prepared for him; but this is so rare, that you soon become accustomed to the sudden intrusion; I have seen persons newly arrived in this country furiously enraged with these unceremonious water-purveyors, on such occasions; but it is a folly, as they never can understand a word you say; but strangers, who do not know the language, always appear to forget this. The *bheestie* is so much in the habit of finding people in bed, that he seldom takes the trouble to look at them. If he suspects that you are rising, he may give two or three grunts, but you cannot detain him long—aware, as you are, of the many leaks from his antiquated sheep-skin. English ladies in India are obliged to conquer, in some degree, their fine sensibilities in such matters. Liable as they are to perpetual intrusions of this kind, they soon become indifferent to the customs of the country, and appear practically to recognise the good sense of Edward the Third's well-known motto.

The *pawney-wallah (pawney*, water—*wallah*, man) is a man upon whom you must keep a sharp eye.—He is not to be trusted alone in an apartment containing small portable articles; and it is the duty of the *muscalche*, or table servant, to attend him in his progress over your bungalow. A friend of mine having occasion to leave her room for a few moments one morning, perceived, upon her return, that a very attractive Delhi brooch had been removed from her toilette-table. The servants were summoned; and suspicion was immediately fixed upon the *bheestie*, who, having been in the room during her temporary absence, was ordered back, to give an account of himself. Of course, he most stoutly denied having touched the missing article. He prostrated himself to the ground, called upon a variety of gods, celestial and terrestrial, to prove his innocence. His kummerband was removed, and his slippers were shaken, and his mouth examined; but no brooch was to be found; and he was about to be dismissed as innocent of the theft, when an accidental derangement of his turban, in the hurry of departure, caused the lost trinket to fall to the floor. The man was sent down to the bazaar-master, and punished; and was banished frcm the district, as a warning to other evil-doers. It should, however, be considered, that, as a class, water-carriers are often exposed to great temptations.

through the culpable carelessness of individuals, or their servants; nor do they often take advantage of their many opportunities of pilfering. Moreover, their civility and willingness to oblige you at all hours, together with their low charges, render them favourites; and the grunting *bheestie* is looked for as regularly every morning at daybreak, as the cold bath, which it is his duty to replenish.

The dergie, or the plain-sewing man, does all your needlework, sitting cross-legged under your verandah. He executes his work beautifully, but must have a pattern to copy; which pattern indeed, if not watched, he is apt to copy too exactly; having been known to introduce a patch into the back of an officer's new uniform, in imitation of a similar disfigurement in the garment sent for a pattern. The *dergie* is the comfort of all ladies who, in their foreign home, either will not, or cannot, ply the needle for themselves. Happy is the man in India who is blest with a wife, who will herself look to the condition of his cotton socks, and other similar matters. I know the blame is always thrown upon the climate and the heat; and it would be unreasonable to be *very* irate even though the *dergie should* have every week a basket or two full of collars or wristbands to patch up; yet, I have often thought, home might have more charms than it appears to have to the Anglo-Indian lady, and the external world less demands upon her time. How often does a wife, who was careful about many things at home—

I speak of that necessary care which does not come under condemnation—shake off all her responsibilities as it respects domestic matters, and fall an easy prey to the indolent habits and self-indulgent customs of this idle country. "India," said a lady to me one day in Bombay, "is a sad school for young wives, and a wretched one for poor husbands." The *dergie* is considered by good judges to be a beautiful needleman; and there are very few articles of dress that he is not able to make up satisfactorily from a pattern. He is honest, and, like many other natives of the east, easily instructed; and he works very quickly with an awkward ivory thimble, pushing the needle *from* him, instead of towards him. He never fixes his work by means of a pin, but keeps it on the stretch, by holding one end of it tightly between the soles of his feet. As he works, he hums some low-toned ditty, and looks the picture of contentment. He usually sits near your drawing-room door, upon a mat, which he spreads out to keep all clean and tidy. His turban he converts into a pincushion; in a hole in the centre of it he deposits the wax with which he liberally coats every needleful of the thread which he uses. The *beating process* already mentioned affords him plenty of business.

The *dergie* is singularly good-tempered. I have seen a lady box his ears—perhaps in a fit of abstraction—for doing his work amiss. He took the affront very good-humouredly, laughed, and appeared amused by the onset of the wrathful fair one; merely saying, as, with the greatest possible composure, he sate down again, to unpick the offending work, "Madam *very* angry this time with poor dergie; but me do it over again, and please angry madam, next time, hopes." The *dergie*, who comes to you about eight o'clock in the morning, brings with him his little brass *chattee* full of his own particular drinking-water, and a few parched grains of corn that have been fried in *ghee*;* and on these viands he dines at one o'clock. After this humble repast, he cleanses his mouth most carefully; gathers a little branch from any neighbouring tree; forms the end of it into a sort of brush; and passes another half hour in polishing with this instrument his pearly teeth. He then taps his forehead two or three times, as if blessing himself, and again sits down upon his mat, to pore over his

*Ghee is a description of clarified butter daily used by the natives of Hindostan, and forms an important article of traffic through a great part of Central India. The manner of preparing it is curious. Each district has, I believe, its own receipt; but the one in common use is as follows. The new milk must be boiled in an earthen pot for two or three hours, after which it is allowed to stand till quite cool, when a little sour milk (tyre) is added to assist in the coagulation. Next day the whole of the milk will be found sufficiently coagulated; when the upper part, to the depth of five or six inches, is to be taken from the mass put into a clean earthen jar to be churned. After churning for about half an hour, a little boiling water is added, when after a little more churning, the butter separates The butter so collected is kept until it becomes rancid, when salt and betle-leaf are added, and then it is potted for use. Churning is a very simple process in the East. A split bamboo is turned round quickly by the hand in the milk, and continued until the butter forms. English families have their butter churned in a bottle with a bamboo through the cork of it; the bottle is shaken with the milk for half an hour.

quiet work, until the sun goes down, and the shadows of night bid him depart. Such is the native *dergie* whose portrait I have sketched from an old friend, who had worked for years for the family with whom I resided. He was a great favourite, and a type of his *caste*.

The services of the *meeta* and *metrane*, male and female sweepers, or, as they are commonly called, *jarra-wallahs*, are indispensable in every bungalow. A few words concerning these poor despised people, may not prove uninteresting to my readers. They excite our sympathy, because they are poor, and have been scouted for ages, nay, abhorred, in India, in consequence of their supposed unfortunate birth and lack of caste. Those who have interested themselves in the early history of the *Chandalas*, (for these people are members of this tribe,) maintain, that they were originally the offspring of a *Sudra*, and a woman of the haughty Brahmin caste. Hence arose the intense dislike which all the Hindoos entertain towards them. They are forbidden to reside in towns, or in any way to associate with those of caste. Their chief occupation consists in carrying away the dead to their place of burning, or burial; in removing the daily accumulations of pestilential, refuse matter, that poison the approach to most houses in the native villages; in digging graves for the carcases of dead animals; in executing criminals; and, in fact, in the most menial and disgusting occupations, in which a man can be engaged. The *meeta* is a sort of hanger-on about your bungalow, and pays his first visit early in the morning, armed with a couple of short-handled brushes, made out of the dried leaves of the plantain, or date palm-tree. He walks round to that side of your dwelling usually occupied as sleeping passages by your domestics, and if they are not astir, he announces his arrival by running the handle of his brush up and down the Venetian shutters outside; thus producing a noise not unlike a watchman's rattle, and generally effectual to the awakening of all the sleepers in the neighbourhood. He sweeps out your rooms in conjunction with the *metrane;* the latter performing all the lowest duties of a chamber-maid; duties which your *ayeh*, from religious motives, will not undertake. Having finished matters within your house, they adjourn to the stables, where they remove from your horses their soiled litter, which, for similar reasons to those which actuated your ayeh, your horse-keepers refuse to touch. Your cooking-houses, and the approaches to your bungalow, are also swept; this being a duty which your *molly*, or gardener, in like manner, refuses to perform. They bring with them a number of baskets, to receive and carry away the rubbish; placing one on the top of another, and carrying away a pillar of them on their heads; a feat which it is worth getting up early to witness, for it is marvellous to see how nicely they poise them. Your other servants avoid these poor people as much as possible; for they will lose caste, they say, if seen even to converse with them; to *touch* them, is thought to be pollution of the very vilest description. They appear, from what I could collect respecting them, to be a quiet race of persons, who gain an honest livelihood in the houses of the wealthy; though the small sum which they receive from each employer per day, would excite the contempt of many a street-sweeper in England. A coarse muslin wrapper round the loins, and falling as low as the knee, where it is tucked up, and a small flat white turban, flat from carrying weights upon it, constitute the whole of the costume worn by these useful, though despised people, who add so much to the comfort of John Bull and his children in India.

Your *gharry-wallah*, or horse-keeper, lives in the stable, with your horses; and it is not unusual to find him, if you peep in at night, fast asleep with his family, by the side of the Arabian. He is a hard-working man, and has to attend you when out visiting. If you are on horseback, he runs after you, and always carries a *chowrie*, or whisk of hairs in his hand, to keep the flies off the animal. If you run a carriage, you put him in livery, and he sits behind you on the step; on such occasions he boasts of being your *syce*, or groom. These stable-men are, generally speaking, an obstinate race; and it is a difficult matter to persuade them to undertake the care of more than one horse. Horses in India always when in stable, have the hinder-legs tethered to a stake driven into the ground; for they are so tormented by insects, that it is dangerous to approach them, unless secured in this manner. As the gharry-wallah and your horses live upon the same sort of corn, (gram,) you must see the latter fed yourself, every day, to ensure them getting their proper allowance, for you can place no confidence in these native servants when out of your sight.

If you want to have an article of jewellery made or repaired, you send for the goldsmith to come and put all to rights. He brings with him his little charcoal furnace, crucibles, and blow-pipe—in fact, everything necessary to melt, mould, or mend; and it is customary to supply yourself with the gold or silver which may be requisite for such operations, and which may be readily purchased; the current coin of the country answering very well, where there is any difficulty in procuring the precious metals. It is excessively amusing to watch the native goldsmith, as he is seated by his fire, and going through the various processes connected with the fusing, or perhaps purifying of the metals. He fans his embers up into a red heat with only a common punkah, which he uses very dexterously. His working-tools are curious, and complicated in their construction, bnt appear to be well adapted for the purposes intended, and satisfy you at once that they were originally designed by no common minds. Not any of the tools that I saw are copies of those manufactured in Birmingham or Sheffield; which, seeing that there are such large importations of these useful instruments into India every year, may seem surprising. The native goldsmith prefers working with tools of Indian manufacture. He is accustomed to them from long use, and the shape is religiously preserved. They suit the feeble grasp of his delicate hand, and though he gets on slowly with some of them, yet time is not to him so valuable as to our own industrious artisan.—He is skilful, and can set you stones very neatly; or, make, from a copy, chains, rings, or brooches, if the pattern be not very difficult. The native jeweller is also a cutter and polisher of diamonds, though he cuts them unscientifically, from the want of proper machinery. Consequently, Indian-cut diamonds are but little esteemed at home; and when they are valuable, and will bear it, are re-cut before they are sent into the London market. Trinkets, and all sorts of jewellery being so much worn by the Indian ladies, our artist makes one of a numerous class, who carry on a very profitable trade in every town and village throughout Hindostan. From him may be purchased the most costly gems; and though to all appearances a poor man, he will often, should you express a wish to purchase any of these adult playthings, pull out from under his gown a dirty roll of linen, in which he has folded an amount of treasure that astonishes you, when spread out to view. Here is a bit of brown paper, with a diamond wrapped up in it, worth fifty pounds; there a ruby, that graced the brow of some maharajah; in another, a portrait of some old king of Delhi, exquisitely painted, and surrounded by brilliants; in another fold, fastened by a pin, is a nose ornament, set with magnificent emeralds. He shows you a ring of plain gold; you examine it, and see nothing particular about it; he smiles—touches a spring—and the ring falls to pieces, and forms a necklace two yards long, that can be returned at pleasure into its originally small compass. You perhaps want to buy a Trinchinopoly chain from him; he does not keep them, but says "he can make you one very like." He squats himself down in a corner of your room; unwinds from his neck some hundred yards or two of fine gold wire; cuts it into proper lengths; fastens sixteen or eighteen ends together; and in a few hours bows himself into your presence, with the chain finished, and all plaited by the nimble fingers of the little dusty, dirty man, whom perhaps you had sent for to solder your teapot-lid. If you supply him with gold or silver when doing anything, it is very necessary to watch him closely, as he is, like too many of his countrymen, given to pilfering. I remember a case in point. A friend of mine had some old epaulettes, which he wished to have melted down, just for the sake of the silver which they contained, and with which he desired to have some trinkets repaired. The village jeweller was sent for, the same man I have taken the liberty of sketching here. He set to work in the usual way, and when the wire was in a fused state, he pulled out a small phial containing a powerful acid, of which he was just going to pour some into the crucible, when my friend arrested his arm, and told him that the acid was quite unnecessary, and the trick not a new one to him. I was a little surprised, and asked, after the jeweller's departure, for an explanation.— The fact is, that when these artists cannot rob you, as they always will do if possible, of a portion of the precious metal, they, as a last chance, pop into the molten mass a little acid, which causes it to boil over, —apparently to their great sorrow; but when they return home, they search the cinders into which the gold or silver has run, and, in this cunning way, rob you before your eyes.

CHAPTER X.

"As Eastern priests in giddy circles run,
And turn their heads to imitate the sun."

Sketch of the Guebres. City of Yezd. Atishgar, and banishment of the Fire-worshippers out of Persia. Their dissent. The Rusmis and Cadmis. Conversation with a Parsee. My friend Nesserwanjee. Love of imitating English customs. Outcasts rejected. How they dispose of their dead. Dockmehs, or Temples of Silence. Religion. Oramanes and Arimanes. The Zendavista. Ormusd and the Great Spirit. Devout Parsees. The water called zor. Sacred cord. The two converts. Sir Jamsetjee Jeejebhoy, his munificent gifts of charity, his knighthood, and opinions of his friends, his wealth and carriages. Lord Keen and the invitation to a ball. Parsee ladies. Town and country house. Visit to Sir Jamsetjee's house in the Fort. Elegant rooms and furniture. Prodigal expenditure at feasts, &c. A bridegroom's folly. Visit to the Burra Babee. Her jewels and diamond necklace. Mourning for the dead. Our salaams, &c., &c.

Having made some allusion to the Giaours, Guebres, Sabrians, Parsees, or Fire-worshippers—for they are all one and the same people—it may, perhaps, not prove uninteresting to those who are not very familiar with the history of this strange sect, if I introduce to their notice one of these remarkable men, and add him to our list of national portraits.—But before we speak of Sir Jamsetjee Jeejebhoy individually, it is necessary that we should take a little journey into Persia. We will not linger among its rose-gardens, for we must pass over sandy deserts and lofty mountains, as fast as our camels will carry us, until we cross the borders of Farsistan, and enter the province of Irak Agemi, whence a guide will conduct us to the caravanzera of Yezd, and the city of which we are in search.

Yezd has long been celebrated for its manufactures. We are delighted with its porcelain works, and long to carry home with us some of those soft rugs and carpets, so much sought after by the luxurious Turks, to supply their harems. The hand-loom is busy at work. Rich silks and showy cottons attract our notice, as we ramble through the close and ill-ventilated bazaars, and foreign merchants, in odd costumes, crowd around us, and dispute the footpath with us. "Dog of an infidel," cries one, as, elbowing his way out of an opium shop, he puffs a cloud of scented tobacco-smoke in our face; "By Allah, that's a Giaour," says another. We have excited curiosity. A short, plump, animal-looking Mussulman, armed with a little brief authority, taps us on the shoulder, and demands our business in the city of Yezd;* and if we cannot satisfactorily prove

* The district of Yezd is, somewhat inconsistently in a geographical point of view, considered as belonging to Irak, for it assuredly makes part of Khorasan. It is an oasis in the vast desert which reaches from the

to him, that we are neither Giaour nor Guebre, he insists upon our paying him at once a sum of money varying from five to fifty rupees, just as he may estimate our ability to comply with his demands. Such is the way in which these hated Mohammedans levy their black-mail upon all poor pilgrims who annually resort hither to pay their vows at the shrine of one whom they detest, and whose name has become a by-word among them. The love of gain, however, has long got the better of their religious scruples; and the fire, which Zoroaster is said to have first kindled in the temple of Yezd, and which is fed with costly wood night and day, by a few unbelievers, who are permitted to live in the city and keep it up, still continues to blaze in spite of persecution. In process of time these Fire-worshippers became a dispersed

Elburz to Kerman. The city is built in a large sandy plain nearly encompassed by hills; but a thinly-inhabited tract in which there are several respectable towns and villages extending in the direction of Ispahan, from which it lies due east. In spite of the dryness of the soil and climate the territory produces good fruits. silk and corn, but not enough of the latter to serve more than forty days' consumption. Yezd, with all these disadvantages is among the most prosperous cities in Persia; and this it owes to its commerce and manufactures. It is one of the great entrepots between the east and west. Caravans from Cabul, Cashmere, Bokhara, Herat, Mushed, Kerman, are met by merchants from Ispahan, Shiraz, Cashan, Teheran and an immense interchange of commodities takes place. On the other hand, its manufactures of silk and other stuffs, its felts, sugar-candy and sweet-meats, command a ready market every where. The population was stated to Captain Christie to be about 50,000 souls, and among them are 300 families of Ghebres or followers of Zoroaster, an industrious and patient race, who in spite of a heavy taxation turn their attention busily to trade and agriculture."—TRAVELS IN KHORASAN.

people; and Mohammedan tyranny is said to have driven out thousands, friendless and destitute, into foreign lands. Numbers of these poor exiles found a shelter in Guzerat. Some were sold as slaves to different Indian princes; and after the death of their leader they were scattered to the four winds of heaven. Wherever they are now met with in Hindostan, they tell you, that they brought with them some of the sacred fire that burns in one of Zoroaster's beloved Atishgahs at Yezd; that in their new home they have erected a temple for its reception and honour; that *Dusturs*, or priests, watch over it; and that no one of a faith different from theirs is permitted to enter the sacred building. Here, however, as elsewhere, the uneasy spirit of dissent has broken the tender ties of kindred and country which originally bound this persecuted sect together; and the Fire-worshippers of India are now divided and subdivided into many jarring parties. The *Rusmiz*, not content with the doctrines which Zoroaster taught them, have imbibed, from long association, many of the popular superstitions of their Hindoo neighbours. Thus, young people, whom curiosity tempted at first to join as spectators, the gaudy and glittering ceremonials of Brahmanism, grew up in time converts to it. The *Cadmiz* alone boast of having preserved pure the faith of their forefathers. It is unnecessary to say, that their religion has sank to an idolatrous worship of the fire and sun: though a Parsee in Bombay told me that he did not worship the sun; for *that* he knew to be folly; but as the sun was the most glorious thing which the Great Spirit had created, he fixed his eyes upon it as he repeated his *Zendavista;* for he knew that God was behind it. When I told him that God was every where, and that he had especially forbidden man to bow down and worship the sun, and moon, and stars, and all the host of heaven; that nothing could displease him more than such worship—he was silent; so I went on, and told him, that one of the great objects England and other christian countries had in view in sending out missionaries to India, was to persuade the Hindoos to forsake the worship of blocks of wood and stone. Here, he interrupted me; and said, in an excited manner, that the Hindoos were a horrid and bad people; pointed out to me all their errors, and appeared thankful that he was not one of them. So prone are we to see the defects of our fellow-creatures, while we shut our eyes to our own. I was about to remind him of the sacred fire which he himself worshipped in the temple, when a sudden thought seemed to flash across his mind.

"You say," he observed, "that you send out Padres to teach the Hindoos not to pray to wood and stone; how is it then, you have so many in England who worship a figure in their temples, just as the Portuguese do here, but I cannot remember the name they give it, or that of the woman, of whom they have so many pictures, and about whom they talk so much." Nesserwanjee had here put to me a rather difficult question. I will not detain my readers with the answer which I gave to his queries. I was at that time, like himself, very young, and I can remember, that I did not satisfy him ; for I found it a topic very difficult to discuss with one who was ignorant of the Word of God and of the plan of salvation. Poor Nesserwanjee! he came to see me almost every evening to learn, as he said, all about the English and the customs of my native land; and to practise upon a pianoforte that belonged to a gentleman who lived in the house in which I resided, and who had, to gratify and encourage native talent, kindly taught him music. He had always a bunch of Mogree flowers for me in the top of his turban, for he knew they would please me. I think I still see his fine handsome face full of smiles as he entered my room, curious to find out if I could spare time "to talk a little with him."—He was a dandy in his dress, for the cotton robe usually worn by the Parsees, he had substituted one made of exquisitely fine cashmere ; the ordinary white socks had been changed for *open-worked silk-stockings*, and the pretty little turned-up slippers had been cast aside for heavy American shoes ; and all this was, as he said, in order to be "like the English."

The Hindoos say that the Parsees of India are outcasts of Persia, but this they indignantly deny, though it is supposed that many of them were driven out in the eighth century. The 29th of September they celebrate in Bombay, as the commencement of their new year, and the day also of their Prophet's birth. They have a curious way of disposing of their dead. The body is carried out on an iron frame, if a poor person, to one of the public *dockmehs*, or temples of silence, the bearers of the corpse having their shoulders tied together by a sacred cord, to scare away the *gins*, or evil spirits, who delight, they say, to flit about the dead on their passage to the tomb. A dog performs the same duty when a Parsee is dying. He sits in the sick chamber, and thus, by his presence, scares away the wicked demons from the bed. The "temples of silence" are large cylindrical buildings, twenty-six feet high, built of solid masonry, and open at the top. They are some miles from the Fort in Bombay, and many of the wealthy Ghebres have private temples of their own. Inclined planes slope down from the walls of the interior, on which are deposited the bodies, loosely wrapped in a linen garment; and as the bones accumulate, they are thrown into a well at the bottom, which has a communication by a subterranean passage, to enable a person to creep in and remove them, when the pit is too full. The bodies so exposed are soon torn to pieces by the fowls of the air, and it is in Persia considered a happy omen if the right eye is devoured first by the carrion vulture.

The Parsees believe that our earth, with its inhabitants, is under the control of the ruling spirits known as Oramanes and Arimanes. Oramanes, or Ormuzd, as he is sometimes called, is worshipped as the originator of all that is good and pure, in heaven and earth; while Arimanes, or Ahriman, is thought to be continually engaged in the dissemination of evil. In the Zendavista, which is one of their rituals of devotion, the resurrection is confidently spoken of: fifty years will be occupied in judgment of the human race. Fire, earth, air, water, is to yield up each the portion they possess of the body of man, which they say, as soon as he dies, enters into these elements; the soul will be re-united to its earthly body, and the juice of the plant Hom, and the milk of a certain bull, will recall the wandering spirit to its home, and man will then live again, and throughout all eternity. Wicked men have, by their doctrine, to undergo a sort of purgatory—a horrible suffering for 3000 years—when Ormuzd will have mercy on them, and permit them to enter into heaven. Ahriman, with all his demons, will in the end be converted, and worship, as ministering angels, the Great Spirit. Strictly speaking, the Parsees have no temples for worshipping in. Their temple is the world; and fire and light, air and water, have each a peculiar adoration paid to them. The *atihsgah*, or fire-temple, is only to protect the sacred flame from extinction or defilement. As fire is worshipped, they never make an improper use of it. For this reason, a fire once lighted in a house is never extinguished, though they will now, I believe, put out a *house on fire*. They will not use fire-arms; and I remember a Parsee, from whom I had purchased some cheroots, refusing to give me fire to light one of them. "My religion will not permit me," he said. Many of the devout Parsees, though they have both money and inclination to travel by sea, and visit foreign countries, will not do so, fearing they should, in a long voyage, pollute the waters they hold so sacred. A holy water, called *zor*, is used by them in driving away bad spirits, and a drop of the venerated juice already spoken of as restoring life to man, is put into the mouth of the new-born babe, and of the dying man, to cleanse them from all impurities. The investiture of young people with the sacred cord and shirt, as a shield against Ahriman, is perhaps one of their most solemn and interesting ceremonies. Altogether, there is much superstition mixed up with their religion, though we find that chastity, honesty, truth, and charity, are required of them, and practised by them. Viewing the Fire-worshippers as a body, we cannot but look upon them as an intelligent, and even enlightened people, when compared with the Hindoos. It may be thought presumption in me, if not in any man, to venture to predict respecting any particular sect in India, that before many years have rolled by, it will be induced, through the preaching of the gospel, to embrace Christianity; yet, I cannot but think, from what I have seen of the Parsees, and of the great anxiety which they have shown to educate their sons, and to have them taught to read and write the English language, that the day is not far distant when their sacred fires will have died out; and when, instead of looking, as they now do, to the genii of the elements for protection, and to the sun as their mediator, they will turn from the visible creature to the Creator, and will look up only to Jesus, the sole Mediator between God and man. A gentleman in Bombay, who had the instruction of several Parsee children, told me, that it was really astonishing how soon they were taught to read and write the English language; and that he would sooner teach half a dozen of these boys, than one heavy European lad. During my residence on that island, there were two Parsee youths who had been induced to embrace Christianity, in Bombay, through the well-directed exertions of one of the Scotch missionaries; but so bitter were the Fire-worshippers against them, that their friends had driven them out, and had denied them the common necessaries of life. It was stated to me, that in consequence of this unexpected animosity, the East India Company had not only to protect, but to support them. They were two fine young men; they regularly attended the Scotch Church, and were, to all, objects of great interest. Some of their enemies said, that they had only changed their religion to please those who had it in their power to procure them good situations, but I have every reason to suppose that such was not the case.

With respect to Zoroaster, the founder or promulgator of the Parsee religion, and the author of the Zendavista, but little is known. Some state, that he was a King of Bactria, and devoted his whole life to the study of magic and astronomy. Others, that he was simply the restorer and reformer of the ancient faith of Persia. To M. du Perron is due the honour of first drawing out from its obscurity, and giving to the world a translation of the Zendavista, a work that had been carefully concealed by the Parsees. It consists, as their traditions assert, of twenty-one nosks or books, of which only one, the Vendidad, is preserved entire. The Abbe Foucher remarks, that the Zendavista "bears exactly the same reference to the books of Zoroaster, that the Romish missals and breviaries do to the Bible."

Having said thus much about the Fire-worshippers in general, we will now turn our attention to Sir Jamsetjee Jeejeebhoy, the patriotic and charitable Parsee, who, by his liberal contributions, has done so much for the improvement of the Island of Bombay; and, whose munificent gift of £500 towards the Bombay subscription for the relief of the suffering Irish in Ireland, during the potatoe famine of 1847, has, no doubt, made his name familiar in England. This striking instance of Oriental liberality is well worthy of being recorded, and requires no comment from me; the noble action speaks for itself. A few months ago, at the opening of the Grand College in Bombay, Sir Jamsetjee Jeejeebhoy intimated, that he had lodged with government, the sum of £1000, on which, interest at six per cent. would be allowed, or about £60 per annum, for assisting, in the purchase of books and instruments, the Alumni, who had distinguished themselves; and £500 beside, which, at a like interest, would afford £30 per annum, for the purchase of prizes for the pupils while in college. "These stimulants," remarks the Editor of the Bombay paper, from which I have extracted the above, "to intellectual exertion, and this culture of general knowledge, are the best auxiliaries in liberating the mind from the bondage of superstition, and in establishing, by the greatest, but most irresistible means, the truths of a Christian and rational religion."

I think it was in the year 1844, that her present Majesty conferred the honour of knighthood upon Sir Jamsetjee, after he had founded the college that bears his name, in Bombay. This was a peculiar mark of the high estimation in which he was held in England; and there were few in Bombay, who, when the news arrived, did not rejoice, and compliment Sir Jamsetjee in no measured terms. It is true, that his Parsee brethren on the island, were a little at a loss to understand what the addition of *Sir*, before their kinsman's name, had to do with his elevation; and they were naturally very curious to know how much money a "Sir" would receive from the kind and good Queen of England; but they had it all explained to them in time, and Sir Jamsetjee Jeejeebhoy is said to wear his honours as a fine old Parsee gentleman should do. Sir Jamsetjee and his son Cursetjee are rich merchants and shipowners in Bombay. From what I could learn during my residence on that island, the bulk of the father's immense wealth had been made in the opium-trade with China, before the "celestial ports" were so effectually opened by the English. Sir Jamsetjee has a prepossessing and benevolent countenance. He is of moderate stature, and a little inclined to corpulency. He dresses in the simple costume of his people, and carefully preserves in its exact shape, the high card-board turban that so distinguishes the Parsees from any other race in India, while it adds so much to their height. Of an evening, Sir Jamsetjee may be seen with his family driving about the fashionable esplanade, in a handsome carriage built in London, after the model of one said to be a favourite with Her Majesty. His splendid horses quite attract attention, for the Parsees pride themselves on being the best judges on the island, of this noble animal, and on their skill in horsemanship.

In 1840, General Sir John Keane, after blowing up the Cabul gate of Ghuznee, and planting the British colours on the battlements of that citadel, returned from Affghanistan by Bombay, on his road to England, to be raised to the peerage, by the title of Baron Keane of Ghuznee and Cappoquin, with a pension of £2,000 a-year. Every one at this time was speaking of the glorious successes of our army in the East, little dreaming of the fearful tragedy that was shortly to be enacted, when thousands of our brave troops were, with their famished and frozen leaders, to perish horribly in the Bolan Pass, mown down like grass before the scythe of the frantic Affghans.

It may appear a little foreign to the subject before us, but I cannot refrain from quoting a passage from

Sir Robert Peel's speech in the House of Commons touching this deplorable event. "When had you before," asked the right honourable baronet, "in the whole cycle of your history, any disaster like that which has befallen you in Affghanistan? a disaster which I admit is not irreparable—a disaster which I trust will be speedily repaired by the spirit and vigour of your councils, and by the gallant exertions of your armies; but when did you ever read in the History of England of such a wholesale slaughter as that which has befallen your forces, and which a private individual reports in every newspaper? Here is what that individual writes:—'My life has been spared in a most wonderful manner, and I am the only European who has escaped from the Cabul army. Two natives only have reached this place, (Jellalabad) making with myself three persons out of an army of thirteen thousand.'"

Sir Jamsetjee Jeejeebhoy, thinking that he must show his satisfaction at our apparent conquests, took advantage of Sir John Keane's temporary sojourn in Bombay, to issue cards of invitation to that officer, his staff, and numbers of the English resident on the island, to a splendid ball which he intended giving in honour of our *great victory*. The invitation was accepted, and a magnificent entertainment was the consequence. Every luxury that wealth could purchase, loaded the tables on this occasion. A gentleman in Bombay told me, that in course of this evening's festivities, a great bustle and stir was observed among the Parsees, friends of the family, who had assembled to witness the ceremonies. There was much whispering and laughing going on, and they had grouped themselves together in little companies near the principal entrance to the ball-room, as if expecting to see something very droll or very curious make its entrance. These circumstances, of course, attracted the attention of the English, and one of the officers jokingly hinted, that perhaps a tame tiger was to be introduced for their amusement. My friend thought, that perhaps Sir John Keane was about to be presented with some substantial remembrance of the worthy Parsee Knight's approval of his late gallant conduct as an officer. The company, however, was not long kept in a state of suspense. Sir Jamsetjee had left the room with his sons, but to re-enter it with his wife leaning upon his arm, and followed by his sons, and their wives and daughters. The surprise of those present can be more easily conceived than described. It was the *first occasion* on which a Parsee lady had ever been seen in public. Sir Jamsetjee had long had his doubts respecting the justice of the selfish custom which deprived the ladies of his, and other Parsee establishments, from enjoying themselves like rational creatures. He had gone to a great expense in giving his daughters a good English education, and he determined upon this occasion, and thenceforward, to show his contempt for such absurd nonsense as the supposed losing of caste or rank, by allowing Parsee ladies to associate with persons of a different faith from his own. He was thus practically acting up to one of the common opinions held among the Parsees; "for God," they say, "delights in the happiness of his creatures;" and they hold it meritorious to enjoy the best of every thing they can obtain. The breaking through, on the part of Sir Jamsetjee's family, of long-established customs so common in India, was a subject of serious conversation among the fire-worshippers of Bombay, and constituted fully a nine-days' wonder among the Hindoo and Mohammedan community. Some thought the ultra-liberal Parsee must be a little out of his reason; others suspected, that he had lost his *Kusti*, or sacred girdle; and all were unanimous as to his having now only *one* soul, and that, of course, the evil one; and they pitied his family, who were led away by his bad spirit. Sir Jamsetjee, however, soon afterwards appeased their anger, and quieted their fears as to his sanity, by building a new Fire Temple on the island at his own expense. His good example in allowing the Parsee ladies their full enjoyment of sweet liberty, was not, I am sorry to say, followed out, as he hoped it might be, in other Parsee families. The Parsee ladies still continue to be shut up in their houses, though many of their husbands have acknowledged to me the folly of the custom; owning that it made them appear in the eyes of strangers little better than Hindoos.

Sir Jamsetjee has a handsome country, as well as a town residence. The latter is situated in Rampart

Row, Fort George. I had the pleasure of going over it one day in company with a few friends, who were particularly desirous to see, if possible, some female branches of the family, who were reported to be extremely fair and beautiful. It is a very large square building, enclosed in front, and separated from the street by a court-yard. After ascending a flight of steps we entered the hall, a good room, with the floor plastered with fine chunam. The walls were hung around with portraits of some celebrated Mandarins, well executed in water-colours, by Chinese artists. We were rather amused at the domestic arrangements of this apartment, and the good use made of it. Seated upon mats in the Oriental posture, were all the mechanics employed by the family, busily engaged in their different occupations. In one corner was a shoemaker, cutting out leather of various colours for slippers. In another was a *dergie*, embroidering pretty little *sadars*, or under-dresses for children, by running lace-patterns into the muslin. A harness-maker was finishing off a saddle; and another man was giving to palanquins a fresh coat of varnish, in anticipation of the rainy season. Indeed, it was quite evident from what we saw here, that Sir Jamsetjee's large family afforded constant employment to numbers of these people. After inspecting every trifle worthy of notice, our conductor, who was a Parsee storekeeper, and, I think a connection of the family, conducted us to the foot of a long staircase, where there was a strong stone built room, having a low door sunk deep in the massive masonry. As this door was bound with iron bands, and secured by three huge padlocks, (Brahmas, no doubt,) our curiosity was a little excited to learn what could possibly be kept inside requiring such precautions for its safe custody, when Merwanjee told us, that the room being fire-proof, all the plate and jewels were deposited here every night; and thief-proof, too, thought I, as we ascended the staircase that terminated in a series of long passages covered over with fine Manilla matting. These passages or promenades, for, in Eastern houses, they are used as such, were well lighted by open spaces like windows without panes, each commanding a view of a pretty garden tastefully constructed in a quadrangle formed by the buildings around it. Here were placed seats of porcelain, stone, and the stumps of trees curiously carved. The first room which we entered was one fitted up in the English style, all the furniture having been manufactured in London. The walls were richly coloured: for paper can never be used in India, as the white ants would eat it up in a few days. Here were portraits of some branches of Sir Jamsetjee's family, painted in oil by an artist who had come out to Bombay on speculation, and who had pocketed five hundred rupees for each picture. The second drawing-room, as we were informed, was furnished in the French style; and if lofty-pier-glasses, statuary, vases of artificial flowers, musical clocks, elegant chandeliers, marble brackets, with groups of alabaster figures on them, Bohemian glass, gilt couches and chairs, are in favour with our continental friends, this room afforded no doubt a good specimen of their taste in domestic decoration. The next and most interesting apartment to us was the Chinese drawing-room. We were delighted with every thing we saw here, as it contained so many beautiful articles brought from China. The whole of the furniture appeared to be made out of papier mache, ivory, or mother-of-pearl. There were three superb folding screens with the most brilliant designs in gold, silver, and pearl-work. The tables were set out with bronze figures of birds, tortoises, Chinese idols, and magnificent Japan jars; one table bore, in a glass-case, a noble silver epergne, representing a plantain tree, with peacocks spreading out their tails under it, that had been presented to Sir Jamsetjee by the merchants of Bombay as a mark of respect to the worthy Knight. Lounging-chairs, sofas, queer little couches, ottomans, and Persian and Turkey rugs, and prayer carpets were distributed about in great profusion, and made one fearful of almost walking upon such beautiful fabrics. We spent some time in this room, the last of the state apartments, if I may so term them. The Parsees, I may observe here, are a very sociable set of people, fond of pleasure and amusement, which after business hours they pursue eagerly, and are extremely liberal and hospitable one towards another. They resemble the Persians in this respect, and are prodigal in the

the expenditure of money for show, or, for the celebration of any particular family event. In celebrating their marriages they are ridiculously profuse in their liberality. Hundreds are invited to the feast; and presents of shawls and other costly things are made to friends in all directions. A bridegroom has been known to expend half his fortune in a public entertainment kept up on the most extravagant scale for three weeks or a month after the ceremony. I was once invited to one of these merry meetings held in a large marquee for want of proper house-accommodation. The amusements consisted of the dancing of *nautch* girls; rose-water sprinklings; making little presents to one another of favourite spices neatly folded up in green leaves; devouring all sorts of confections for which the city of Yezd is so celebrated; and invoking blessings upon the newly-married people in songs that were certainly not very musical. We were now anxious to get a peep if possible at that portion of this large house occupied by Sir Jamsetjee's family; and having obtained permission, we inspected some of the dormitories, which we found to be comfortable and well-ventilated rooms, containing the conveniences usually found in such apartments at home. Merwanjee took us into a long dining-hall, where a table was set out for some repast. Like the Hindoos the Parsees are very particular about eating and drinking out of any vessel that has been defiled by one of a different faith, and they object to share in the cup of one of their own people, fearing that by so doing they may partake of their sins. The hare, dog, vulture, and some other birds and beasts of prey are forbidden food, though dogs and cocks have a sacred character attached to them. All poisonous reptiles they instantly deprive of life, as creatures which Ahriman delights to send forth as messengers of his evil intentions towards man. We followed Merwanjee through a series of other rooms, and up another flight of stairs out on to the flat roof, where we enjoyed a most splendid view of the whole island of Bombay. Seats were placed on the leads for the accommodation of the ladies, who retire hither morning and evening to pray, and to read over their book of Zendavista, and study the Dabistan, and the Dassateer, as the two latter contain a history of various superstitions commonly practised among them, and a sketch of the life of one Hoshung, who, they say, first worshipped the true fire. Upon our return, Merwanjee, at our request, introduced us to a part of Sir Jamsetjee's family. Upon entering their private room we found an old lady and three young looking girls sitting close together, upon low chairs, with their feet tucked under them; but we could not discover that they had been engaged in any employment, for Eastern ladies have no resources within themselves. The rich, generally speaking are taught nothing, and are kept in a sad state of ignorance; all they know of the world is principally gleaned from story-tellers, or from the foolish traditions handed down by the Dustoors, Mobads, and Herboods—orders of the priesthood among the Parsees.

Sir Jamsetjee's family are certainly an exception to this rule, for both his sons and daughters have been well educated. The *burra-babee* or old lady, appeared delighted to find that one of our party (a lady) could converse freely with her in Hindostanee. She wore a crimson *sarree*, that had been put on gracefully over her head, and hid everything in its folds, save two small hands, that were loaded with beautiful rings; for truly "rich and rare were the gems she wore," and which sparkled and glittered all over her person. Her nose ornament had a very large pearl on it, but sadly disfigured that prominent feature on one side. She appeared a little anxious I thought to display her ornaments, baubles which are cast aside by the Anglo-Indian lady in this country as being too common, or too much like the natives, and seeing that we admired a fine emerald on her finger, she unfastened from under her *sarree*, at Merwanjee's suggestion, a sort of hoop-necklace set with the largest diamonds I ever remember seeing; and the splendid string of jewels was handed about for us all to examine. The ladies were particularly in love with the beauty of the brilliants, and upon returning the necklace, said it must have cost a very large sum of money. The *burra-babee* smiled as she clasped it round her wrinkled neck, and remarked, that it was only *her every day necklace*; and that she did not wear her very good ones except on festive occasions. Her companions were very shy, and not at all disposed to enter into conversation—one of them, who was attired in a white *sarree*, and had a very melancholy cast of countenance, had retired to a recess near the window soon after we had entered the room; upon inquiry, we learned that she was the daughter-in-law of the chatty old dame, and had just lost her second boy; who a few days before had been placed by the side of his little brother in the Temple of Silence, belonging to the family. We could scarcely believe that so young a creature had already been the mother of two children. "She is mourning over them very bad," said Merwanjee; and fearing that by prolonging our stay we might be intruding upon this sorrowing one, we made our low salaams to the *burra bubee;* and thus ended an agreeable visit to the house of Sir Jamsetjee Jeejeebhoy.

CHAPTER XI.

"I will buy with you, sell with you, talk with you, walk with you, and so following; but I will not eat with you, drink with you, or pray with you."

MERCHANT OF VENICE, Scene 3d, Act 1.

Bombay Jews, are they true Israelites? Arabian and White Jews. My opposite neighbours. Stolen peeps across the street. Their habits, dress, and mode of spending their time. My favourite boy. His dress and ayeh. Scene changes. Few words about a cat and a dog. Tasso deserts me. Hospital for animals, and belief in the transmigration of souls. Tasso's unfaithfulness. Little dogs have queer fancies. Six o'clock at the Jewish family's house. Prayers and songs and sweet music. My last look at the window. Sorrow at separation from the Jewish child. Their innocent and happy life, &c., &c.

THE Jews in Bombay constitute rather a large item in the population.* Five or six thousand have settled

* The results of the census taken in May, 1849, have been published; and it appears, that in the Island of Bombay, comprising in all twenty square miles of ground—four-fifths, at least, of which are uninhabitable swamp or rock—there are in all no fewer than 566,119 inhabitants, of whom 354,090 are males, and 212,029 females. Of these, 6,936 are Brahmins, 289,995 are of other castes of Hindoos; 1,902 are Jains; 124,155 are Mohammedans; 114,698 Parsees; 1,132 Jews; 7,456 native Christians; 1,333 Indo-Britons; 5,417 Indo-Portuguese; 5,088 pure

down in the city and neighbourhood, and obtain for the most part an honest livelihood, as house-builders, carpenters, and cultivators of the soil. That a Jew should be thus employed may appear singular to many who are familiar with their history, and their known dislike to anything like manual labour; for who ever heard, among ourselves, of a Jewish farmer, or a Jewish carpenter? We are tempted, however, to doubt the *purity* of the race met with in all the commercial towns in India; and to suppose that they, like the Parsees, Mohammedans, and other interlopers, have degenerated, from long association with a people at total variance with anything like Christianity. The following brief account given of the Jews in Bombay, may, perhaps, throw some light on this interesting subject, and bear us out in the idea, that they are a mixed people, and not the pure race of Hebrews met with in Poland, Germany, or in the corners of the dingy second-hand shops of Holywell Street, London, where these exiles from "Vaderland" buy, sell, and get gain, and do not, so far as we are able to learn, trouble themselves much about the realization of the prophecy that will one day certainly restore them to Palestine. Let us, however, remember that our own sacred Scriptures pointedly make known to us that kindness and respect towards this ancient and peculiar people is most acceptable

Europeans; 889 Siddees, Negroes, and Africans; and 7,118 of other castes unspecified. From this census we learn, that the Europeans are less than one in a hundred of the whole population.

in the sight of God; and though the veil may still be upon their hearts, they are the chosen ones of the Almighty, for "blessing is for them that bless them, and cursing for them that curse them."

A writer, in an Indian periodical (*Dynanodaya,*) informs us, that "Some of the Jews in Bombay have more recently come from Arabia, and are called White Jews. Some have come from Cochin, and are called Black Jews; but by far the greater portion who have settled in this country, and to whom Mahratta is the vernacular language, are called Israelites, or Beni Israel. When their ancestors arrived here, is not certainly known. They say, it was about 1600 years ago, that the ship in which they came was wrecked, and that seven men and seven women, who escaped, settled at Nagao (some thirty miles to the south-east of Bombay). They were, at one time, generally engaged in the manufacture of oil, but at present many of them are masons, carpenters, cultivators," &c. The writer goes on to say, that when the missionaries first came out to the Island of Bombay, (thirty or forty years ago,) the Israelites were generally unable to read, and even almost wholly ignorant of their own Scriptures; that they had generally ceased to observe the Sabbath as a day of rest, and "*and were, in many respects, conformed to the customs of their Hindoo and Mohammedan neighbours.*" It is stated, in a printed journal of the earlier missionaries, that the magistrates described them at that time as being the most drunken and troublesome people on the island. The missionaries, it appears from the author whom I have taken the liberty of quoting, have from the first taken a deep interest in the Israelites or Jews. They early established among them schools, in which both sexes were taught to read and write. They furnished them with the Bible, translated into the vernacular language; and instructed several of them in Hebrew, so that they might be able to refer to the original Scriptures. The consequence of this was, that the Jews forsook many of those things which, on becoming acquainted with the Scriptures, they had found to be forbidden; and that they have greatly advanced in intelligence, wealth, morality, and general respectability. Such is the pleasing account given of the poor Jews in Bombay; and we cannot be surprised, that the missionaries should have first turned their earnest attention to them, when they found that this remnant of a once highly-favoured people had sunk so low as to have forgotten the God of their fathers, and to have turned to worshipping the idols of Brahminism. The dress of the Jews in Bombay differs but little from the costume worn by other Eastern people. Their robes are fuller, and of a superior texture. The men, generally speaking, attract the attention of a stranger, by their commanding figures, and thoughtful and expressive features. They have two regular synagogues in Bombay, and one at Revadunda, where they read the Scriptures in Hebrew and Mahratta. In the Fort they have two private houses, where public worship is held.

On the sea-shore of an evening, I have observed many Jews offering up their prayers among the numbers of different castes who resort thither for that purpose; and, like Jacob of old, worshipping their Creator, leaning on the top of their staff.

A family of Arabian, or white Jews, resided in a narrow street directly opposite the house in which I lodged; and as my sitting-room was pretty lofty, I had daily opportunities of observing this little colony of Israelites from my window, and was often amused by the way in which the female portion of this establishment passed their time. As their Venetian shutters were kept wide open all day, I could, without being observed by them, see distinctly into their principal sitting-room; and even if I were detected casting furtive glances across the street, my Jewish neighbours appeared quite indifferent about the matter. This careless indifference about being overlooked, at times induced me to suppose that it was possible my name was familiar to them, and that they were pleased that one of their own religion had taken up his quarters so near them. But of course this is merely conjectural, though I believe they knew my Jewish sounding cognomen. They were seldom astir before I returned from my morning's walk, and precisely at nine o'clock the master of the house went out on his daily business; but before leaving the step, he would turn round to place the palms of his hands upon the door posts, to bless, as I fancied, the dwelling and its inhabitants; or, it might be done in commemoration of the Passover. This he did regularly, and with an air of apparent solemnity; his lips, as I could detect, seemed moved in the utterance of words that were inaudible to me. He wore a patriarchal-looking beard, that swept far down his white robes; and was particularly neat and cleanly in his personal appearance. His thick cumbrous turban was folded with taste, but his bright orange-coloured slippers being cut much lower than those usually worn by the Hindoos, were so loose upon his feet as to oblige him to shuffle along to keep them on at all, as he walked. His lady seldom went from home; and when she did, it was to take a little exercise in a covered *shigram*; on which rare occasions she wore a dark muslin mask over her face, as the Egyptian women do. Her whole day appeared to me to be exhausted in the care of a lovely cherub-boy, about two years old, whom she nursed and played with for hours together upon a low settee, near the window. Never were a mother's affections more concentrated in one earthly object than hers were in this sweet child; he was indeed "the ocean to the river of her thoughts." About ten o'clock, and after their breakfast of rice, fruits, and chocolate, the old ayeh was called up, to undress our little friend. First, he was placed full stretch upon a large soft pillow, to be champooed by his nurse; an operation that appeared to give him excessive pleasure; for it was done so gently, and mixed up with so many kisses, that he would toss his plump little legs about and laugh so heartily, that I was generally soon aware what was going on opposite. When this was over, he fell fast asleep after his exertions; and, with his tawny skin, resembled an exquisite piece of chiseled marble, tinged with the yellow hue of age. As he lay where the morning breeze could blow softly over him, hushed in the deep slumber of happy innocence, with the fond mother watching by his side, I thought I had never seen so sweet a group; Canova might have chosen it for a study. Sometimes the child was dressed up in the most extravagant finery; gold bangles were clasped round his arms, and anklets set with glittering stones were jingling about his feet; a necklace of gold-coins, three or four deep, were thrown over his fat little shoulders, and he was then put into a nondescript red silk dress, and spangled skull-cap, with a long streaming tassel to it; and all this was done to please the father, on his return.

After tiffin was over, the scene was changed. The only son was then undressed, and dropped into a sort of hammock, suspended in the room where the ayeh, during the absence of the mother, had again to punkah him to sleep, and to amuse herself by killing the musquitoes that annoyed him. There was, however, another object that shared, in some measure, the affections of the Israelitish woman; and this was a very large and beautiful cat, which, like most of his tribe, was fond of wandering from home, and giving trouble to his owners. He was covered with a long, curly, cream-coloured fur; a fine specimen of the

Persian breed; and as he sat purring under a jalousie that projected far over the window, I was often amused to see the strange variety of cats that came to visit and admire him. They all had a foreign air about them, and usually made their appearance on the roof of the house, whence they would peep over curiously, to ascertain first whether Sajee were at his accustomed post before leaping down upon the jalousie and paying their respects to him. Thus it was not uncommon to see five or six sitting sedately together on the window sill, eying every person that passed in the street below. Some were partly dressed up like the monkeys that accompany our barrel-organ boys; and one that was the property of a little Pondicherry Frenchman, next door, was half-shaved, and ornamented with tri-colour ribbons. Puss was as fond of the baby as its mother was; and, whenever he could do it unnoticed, he would steal into the hammock, and famous romps they would have together.

One morning, poor Sajee was missing; servants were sent in all directions to search for him; but in vain. They came early over to my house, to know if I had seen him from my window; but I could give them no information; unless it were, that I had myself experienced a somewhat similar loss, by the disappearance of a small spaniel, which I had brought over with me to the country; and that I strongly suspected they both had been stolen. Tasso, soon after his arrival with me in India, suffered much from frightful fits, occasioned by a degree of heat to which he had never been accustomed. Curious to say, in a short time, he cast his warm English coat, which was replaced by a much thinner covering; and after this salutary change, his fits entirely left him, and the poor fellow recovered his wonted health and animation; and life once more appeared to afford him real enjoyment. The natives understood his complaint; and when his fits attacked him in the street, and he would come suddenly to a full stop for a second or two, and then running violently round in a circle, would drop down, foaming and panting, upon the pavement, convulsed in every limb, they would run into their houses, and bring out large vessels of water to throw over him—an operation which, though it brought him round again, occasioned the poor creature a degree of suffering that it was painful to witness; and I often regretted having brought him out. The kindness shown to my dog must be attributed to the belief of the natives in the transmigration of souls; a belief which induces them to protect and cherish all animals alike. On the following day, the Jew sent over his *bote salam* to me, with the pleasing intelligence, that his favourite cat had been discovered at the native hospital for the preservation of animals; and that my dog, Tasso, had been seen there, enjoying himself in the society of Pariahs, baboons, and long-tailed monkeys; adding, moreover, that if I sent one rupee, with a person who could identify him, to pay for his board and lodging, he would be immediately restored to me. Upon learning this, I despatched my boy, with the required fee in his pocket, to effect Tasso's release; and a few hours afterwards, I had the pleasure of once more patting my old fellow-traveller on the back. He was in excellent condition, and must have been living on the fat of the land; indeed, generally, these imprisoned animals have plenty of food, and are well taken care of. Whether it were the remembrance of his former good quarters and odd associates, by which the dog was actuated, I cannot tell—but Pedro, my boy, came into my sitting-room a few mornings afterwards, and with a woe-begone countenance informed me, that "that little dog like hospital so much, he go again;" and sure enough, Tasso had slipped his collar, and made his escape. To shew that dogs do take strange fancies for animals of a species different from their own, I need only mention a case where a pet poodle in my possession, in England, passed the greater part of every day in company with a monkey that was kept chained in a large yard. They would play together for hours, and the monkey would put his arms round the neck of the poodle, and nurse it as if it had been one of its own offspring. This great intimacy continued for some months, until the monkey was sent away for pulling the slates off an out-building. As I was not in a position to pay a rupee every week for a day or two of Tasso's company, I thought I had better make a present of him to this Hindoo Zoological Society; and, unless he have gone to that bourne from whence no *little dogs* return, I have no doubt but, that at this moment, my brown spaniel, which was born and educated in the Isle of Man, might be recognized in this hospital near Bombay.

But to return to our Jewish friends. Six o'clock saw the happy family again re-united; and at this hour the shutters were finally closed for the night, and the sound of prayer ascended to the Giver of all good, for the mercies of the past day. Although I could not see him, it was impossible to mistake the voice of the father, or the sacred service in which he was engaged. The daily duty ended, and supper over, the mother would sing, accompanying her voice, one of the sweetest I ever heard, with the Spanish guitar; and, as they generally sate up late, I often heard, on awakening in the night, the sweet, pensive airs she used to play; for, unlike the generality of the children of Israel, she could sing the songs of Zion in a strange land.

Eight months had rolled by, and the day at length arrived on which I was to leave this neighbourhood. I took a last parting look at the window where the little boy was wont to amuse me, but I was disappointed. He, who had so long engaged my affection, was not there; and as I turned out of the narrow, close street, I was surprised to find how much I had loved him. A long and dangerous illness, with fifteen weeks' confinement to my room, may, in some measure, account to the reader for the great interest which I took in this Hebrew family. They had often intimated by signs to me, the pleasure they experienced in seeing me once again at my accustomed post; and the poor mother would at times shake her head, as if grieved to see the long thin face that sickness had so reduced; for she knew that I loved her only child, and I am certain that she rejoiced in my recovery. The happy and innocent life which they appeared to lead, contributed, with many other little circumstances which I had remarked during this long season of suffering and trial, to leave a pleasing impression of the Jewish domestic character upon my mind; and for years afterwards I often fancied, during the still hours of night, that I heard the warbling voice of the Israelitish woman.

CHAPTER XII.

Then am I to leave thee! and must we soon part?
Yet time shall not banish past hours from my heart,
Remembrance shall call them, though oceans divide,
And memory shall point to what distance must hide.

A canter over the sands. Government house at Malabar Point and Parell. Unhealthy situation. Island of Salsette, its Antiquities not a part of the Infanta's dowry. Village of Walka-es-Warree. Tanks, priests and people there. Infatuated mendicants. A few words on Ablutions. Palma Christi, or Castor Oil Tree. Bundarres. My visit to the Toddy Drawers. Silence in the woods. Hour and mode of collecting toddy, or Palm-wine. The Cathedral of Bombay. Punkahs, and short and long services. The dead quickly buried. Jackal resurrectionists. Sudden deaths. A night visit from a Ramoosey Borah. Bores and pedlars. My robbery and Pedro's escape. The cook's Portuguese blessings. Bombay police, a useless body. Public suspicions and opinions. Investigation and awful revelations, &c. Conclusion, &c., &c., &c.

A DELIGHTFUL canter over the fine smooth sands carries you, in about an hour, from Fort George to a picturesque road that winds among broken rocks, ornamental bungalows, and dense woods, up to Malabar Hill. This very elevated promontory runs out in a south-westerly direction, like its opposite neighbour, Colabah, but does not extend so far into the ocean.

It forms the western boundary of Back Bay. On its extreme point, and exposed to every breeze that steals over the island, a pretty-looking house rather in the cottage style, had been built for the governor of Bombay to reside in, during the hot season of the year; a telegraphic communication being kept up between the cottage, and the castle in the Fort. The principal residence of the governor is at Parell, and is situated in a more central part of the island. This residence is a handsome-looking building, and contains some noble reception-rooms. It was originally a church belonging to the order of Jesuits, and was purchased by the East India Company for its present purpose. Its low and swampy park, however, and the unhealthy character of its neighbourhood during the monsoons, rendered it not so desirable a situation as had been anticipated. A good road of a few miles in extent takes you from Parell to the causeway that connects Bombay with Salsette. This latter island has some hills of considerable elevation clothed with brushwood to their summits. Tanna and Gorabunda are the principal towns; and are peopled by the descendants of Portuguese families. One of the hills is perforated by excavations cut into the rock, known as the temple-caves of Kennery, and well worth a visit of inspection. The most remarkable is a Bhuddist temple fifty feet long by twenty wide, where a colossal statue of Bhudda, with his hands raised in supplication, is on the east side of a lofty portico. It does not appear that this island was included in the marriage contract already mentioned, for after the surrender of Bombay, the Portuguese still persisted in retaining it, until 1773 when, during the confusion of a civil war which followed the assassination of Narrain Row, the principal fort was stormed by the English, who have ever since retained it undisturbed. This island supplies Bombay with rice, sugar, fruit, sheep, and many other very valuable commodities, and is about twenty miles in length. The views from Malabar Hill and point are truly enchanting. Looking down the rugged sides of this rock, where the Tara and other palms grow spontaneously, the eye rests for a moment upon the deep blue waters which gently lave its base, and which are dotted here and there by odd-shaped coasting-vessels, tacking about the bay, or running ashore on the opposite banks, to discharge their timber cargoes. The view from the point comprehends a vast extent of the Indian ocean and numerous lovely looking-islands; but distant hills that overtop one another shut in the prospect towards the north-east, and form a grand and noble range. We pass on our road a large native village called Walka-es-warre, that is said to contain a population of some three thousand souls. This village has but little to recommend it, for the streets are close and offensive, from the dirty character of the inhabitants; though I have often been amused in passing through it of an evening, by watching the Banian merchants sitting in front of their shops, the business of the day being over, intently engaged in the intricacies of a game of chess; each player had a little crowd around him, who were watching the moves as if each had a large stake set upon the result. Chess is a favourite game with the Hindoos and Mussulmans, and I believe we have to thank the former for its introduction into England. A work explanatory of this Indian amusement, published some years ago in Bombay by a native, lays down rules, which vary but little from those in use among ourselves. The village of Walka-es-warre is rather celebrated for its old Temple, and for the traditional sanctity attached to it by the idle Brahmins, who reap at certain festive seasons of the year their accustomed rich harvest. This temple stands at the head of a fine sheet of water, near to which is a commodious *durrum Saulah*, for the shelter of the pilgrims and travellers, who, during the rains and at their termination, resort hither to bathe in this pool of Bethesda. On such days the steps leading down to it are thronged with the lame, the halt, and the blind, waiting, not for the moving of the waters, but for some kind friend to push them in and give them a good washing; for the filthy and wretched appearance of some of these infatuated mendicants makes this quite an act of charity.

I may here observe to my younger readers, that ablutions occupy an important part in all Brahminical ceremonials. The poor Hindoo, whose bodily infirmities forbid his crawling across the country, or whose limited means will not afford him a conveyance that might carry him to that holy stream which, as he is taught to believe can wash away all sins, is permitted by the rules of his religion, to bathe in the nearest sacred river to his own residence, and it shall be accounted unto him for righteousness. In so doing, however, he must earnestly entreat the Ganges to make this ablution as effective as it would have been, if performed in its own waters, so that he may be freed from all impurities of flesh and spirit. The Mohammedans are even more particular about these observances than the Hindoos: for if really orthodox, they wash after every little work which they perform. They are, however, a very mixed sect in India, and it would be a difficult matter to discover what creed some of them profess.

I saw outside the walls of this village some luxuriant specimens of the tree whose seeds produce our castor-oil (Palma Christi). This showy and beautiful annual, as I need scarcely remark, is indigenous to the soil of Hindostan. The leaves, which bear a striking resemblance to those of the vine, are of a fine bluish green, and the flowers have long stamens of a purplish hue. The capsule, or seed-vessel, as it approaches maturity, puts on a brilliant crimson tinge, and is covered with an armour of short spines, like the horse-chesnut. The seeds, the most useful part of the tree, are quite black; and each has a little cell of its own, whence, when fully ripe, it is shot out by the sudden expansion of its case. These trees seldom attain a height beyond twelve feet; and as they are so ornamental, and easily cultivated, they are frequently introduced, in India, into gardens and shrubberies, for their beauty alone. The expressed oil, which is very fluid in warm climates, is burnt in the lamps of the natives, producing a fine clear light, and not much smoke or smell.

Sauntering one evening in this district, I thought I would pay a visit to some of the *bundarries*, or toddy drawers, and inspect the process of collecting the palm-wine. Having tied my *tattoo* under a spreading tree by the road-side, I got over a low fence, and made my way into a vast *tope*, or plantation of palms; being preceded by a small party of drawers, bearing upon their shoulders three or four large red burnt *chatties* to contain the toddy. The fierce sun was sinking low in the west, and shot its glorious rays under the leafy canopy above us, which was so close and thick as scarcely to permit us to see the least patch of sky overhead. The land breeze whispered through the forest as we walked along, noiselessly, over the withered accumulation of centuries of fallen leaves and bark, and surveyed the long aisles formed by the mighty monarchs of the Eastern vegetable world. There was a strange solitude about the place, broken in upon, occasionally, by some heavy bird that flapped down upon the crowned top of a palm, where it soon hid its head under its wing, and was at rest. We soon reached the scene of action; and casting my eyes up to the tops of the trees, I saw that each of them had a vessel tied under its leaves. To empty these vessels of the exuded juice that had collected since the morning, was the purpose of my companion's present visit. One of the men squatted down on the ground, to fasten his kummerband securely about him, (for they can do nothing in India standing up,) and after taking off his turban, and twisting the lock of hair on the top of his head into a knot, and cracking all the joints of his fingers, he placed a strap around his own body, and the tree which he was about to ascend, and then threw it with much dexterity over the first step cut in the bark; and thus, by a series of movements, throwing the strap successively over each step above him, he was not long in reaching the *chattie* at the top; the height being some ninety or a hundred feet from the ground. Having first made a secure seat of the strap, he untied the cord that fastened the vessel to that part of the tree whence the bruised flower-stem, from which the juice flows, could hang into it; and tying a long *coir* rope round its rim, cautiously lowered it down, with its contents, to the *bundarries* below, to be emptied by them into one of the vessels which they had brought with them. This being done; at a given signal he hauled it up again, and after probing the wound afresh with a knife, and securing the *chattie* once more in its place, he descended cautiously, and at a slower pace than that at which he went up. He appeared to be a little fatigued by his exertions, and gave the strap to another, who proceeded to collect the toddy from the next tree; and so they each ascended in their turn.—

Some of the old palm-trees, that have been sixty or seventy years under the knife-operation, groan and bend fearfully, as the climbers approach the top; but they say there is no danger, as the south-west monsoon generally blows down all the palms which, in consequence of age, will not bear the weight of a man; and I believe it is very rarely that an accident occurs. I was very anxious to taste some of the fresh-drawn toddy, but, from my poor knowledge of the language, had some difficulty in making my wishes understood. One of the elder men, however, as soon as he comprehended my signs, shook his head, saying, at the same time, "*Chattie na saib, chattie na saib;*" and it struck me at once that I should defile the vessel if I drank out of it, and that he had no other to give me; so I made a cup of my hand, and presented to him this ancient drinking-vessel, which he immediately filled with toddy, and repeated the draught until I was satisfied. The palm-wine is the same grateful beverage which, in India, they hawk through the streets for sale, every morning before sunrise; for it is only fit to drink for an hour or two after being collected, fermentation rapidly taking place, and converting it into an intoxicating fluid, which, by distillation, yields the well-known spirit called arrack. As a return for the old man's kindness, I put into his hands an anna, with which he was wonderfully delighted—making me several profound salaams, and grinning after each bow, to evince the pleasure he felt.

In some districts, where the palm-trees are very

close together, they are connected together by ropes, so as to enable the toddy-drawers to go from one to another, without the trouble of descending. I have often felt nervous and dizzy in seeing the drawers ascend some of the towering cocoa-nut trees that stand alone in the Fort, or on Colabah, for it really appears to be a very dangerous exploit. But they are accustomed to it from childhood, and their bare and flexible feet have a safe hold in each of the little steps that are notched into the bark, every three or four feet from the bottom to the top. It was quite dusk before I was again seated on my *tattoo*; and as it was the first time I had strayed so far from home in this direction, I had not proceeded half a mile on my way back, before I discovered that I had lost my way, and that instead of advancing, as I thought, down to the shore, I was cantering just in a contrary direction across the island. At last I halted opposite some huts by the roadside; and turning the tattoo's nose into the open door-way of one, in which I saw a party sitting cooking round a fire, inquired the road to the esplanade, or Fort George, in the best Hindostanee I could muster; but I might as well have addressed them in Welch or German, for anything they could understand. The grown-up people stared at me as if I were a robber, and some children who were asleep in a corner, hearing the chattering, put their heads up above the rags that covered them, and seeing the pony's nose inside the door, burst out into immoderate fits of laughter, in which the little black wretches persisted, until my patience being exhausted, I turned the pony out into the road, not knowing which way to turn. I threw the reins over old Deesa's neck, and giving him a pretty smart cut, left him to take me whithersoever he listed. He put his nose down to the ground, snorted once or twice, and then set off, as hard as he could go down a long lane, where the trees hung over so thick that I had to take my hat off, and hold my head down upon his shoulders to prevent its being knocked off, and even with these precautions I got well lashed by the branches before I found myself going down a long street in the new town. Deesa did not slacken his pace until he turned a corner, and came to a full stop opposite a Portuguese spirit-store and dancing room, from whence proceeded the sounds of vile music and boisterous merriment; crowds were going in sober, and coming out mad and furious with strong drink. I had fortunately not to wait long in this polluted atmosphere, before I detected the face of a boy whom I knew, and who was the servant of a gentleman in the Fort. He told me I was three miles yet from home, and if I would not tell his master where I had seen him, he would get me a guide. I was so tired, that I would have made him any promise, however absurd. A *chokra*, or errand-runner, was soon procured, as well as a palanquin, and giving him the pony to follow after me, in about an hour and a half I found myself at home, and just in time to save from the trouble of setting out in search of me, two servants, who had kindly armed themselves with lanterns and sticks, and other little comforts, and who had obviously intended to make a night of it. So terminated my first visit to the Toddy-drawers.

During my residence in Bombay, I had frequent opportunities of attending divine service in the Cathedral, and was often struck by the smallness of the congregation assembled there on the Sabbath-day, particularly of an afternoon. This sad neglect did not arise from any lack of earnestness on the part of those who laboured in Bombay, as faithful ministers of Christ. The bishop, (Dr. Carr,) often preached, and his sermons, so far as my poor judgment could decide, were sound, eloquent, and impressive discourses; from which few could rise without feeling that they had in some measure been improved by them. Yet, what rows of empty pews did he and others, Sunday after Sunday, preach to! Nay, even of a morning, exclusive of the military, who are, in fact, compelled to attend, how few were the civilians collected in this house dedicated to the worship of the Most High! It is true, there are other places for Christian worship in Bombay, for this island lacks nothing in this respect; but they all wore a vacant aspect, with the exception of the Scotch Church; yet there are, I should imagine, a sufficient number of Protestants resident in Bombay, to fill, even to overflowing, all the churches and chapels on the island, without any addition from the large amount of European shipping constantly riding at anchor in the harbour. A visitor is struck upon entering the cathedral to see so many of the natives collected around its doors. Some peeping curiously in, as if a novel ceremony were going forward; while the children were evidently attracted by the solemn music proceeding from a fine organ. What a desire one felt to take in along with one, these poor little idolaters, and let them taste, if possible, of that living water, that they might thirst no more! What a desire one felt to fill, from the thronged streets, those empty benches which professing Christians had deserted; so that the word there preached might not be lost, and that they who had left kindred and country to come out here to labour in the gospel, might not feel that they laboured almost in vain!

Large punkahs, ten and twelve feet long, are suspended over the body of the cathedral, and kept in continual motion by *coolies* outside the building, who pull a cord which is attached to the fans and carried over a pulley through the window opposite; so that a grateful current of air is kept in circulation. These punkahs just clear the heads of the congregation when standing up; and by their novelty, at first rather diverted my attention, especially if there happened to be a very tall person under them. A small punkah is also suspended in front of the pulpit and reading-desk: for it is impossible during the hot season to remain long with any comfort without this appliance. There are at the west end of the cathedral a few monuments and statues that have been erected to commemorate distinguished officers, who have died in this presidency. How young were the ages recorded on many of them! But however pleasing it may be to see these mementoes of affection reared in our churches at home, their introduction into such places in India cannot but be regretted and condemned; since it is difficult, as I found, to persuade the ignorant natives, that we do not worship the individuals thus commemorated, seeing that we erect their monuments in our temples, and enshrine their stone figures in our sacred places. Surely with such acute observers as the Hindoos, we ought to avoid what to them may be the appearance of evil.

The Cathedral in Fort George consists of a nave and two short side aisles, supported by handsome and polished chunam columns. The tower rises to a good height, and serves, I believe, as a landmark for mariners. The whole structure, with a small burial-ground, is neatly enclosed with an iron railing, and is kept in good order. The church service, after one of the introductory sentences, commences with the litany in the hot season, for the weather is so oppressive that it is scarcely possible to sit long in a place of worship. The prayer used, during the sitting of that august body, for the high court of parliament, has been adapted in the following manner:—"Most gracious God, we humbly beseech thee, as for the empire in general, so more especially for British India; for the governor general, the governor, the supreme courts of judicature, and all that are put in authority, that thou wouldst be pleased," &c. &c.

As within the tropics decomposition advances with fearful rapidity, a hasty burial of the dead is absolutely necessary for the safety of the living. Graves are dug very deep, to prevent the horrible bandicoots and other midnight prowling animals, from rifling them of their contents; and in some districts which I have visited in the interior of the country, it was necessary to place heavy stones over the coffins, or the jackals would have acted the part of resurrectionists, and carried away your departed friend. I have often thought, that this exhumation of the dead by wild animals, so common in India, unless great precautions are taken, may have had originally something to do with the Hindoo custom of burning the bodies of the departed.

Sudden deaths are not uncommon in Bombay, and dysentery carries off its hundreds annually from among the ill-fed and ill-clothed pauper population. Few Europeans escape its attack; but the treatment of this disease in India, by our army surgeons, like many other things in the present day, has undergone a change for the better. Formerly our troops in the East were said to be fairly poisoned by the enormous doses of calomel exhibited in this disease. An old army surgeon states, that it was no uncommon thing for an individual to take before he died eight or nine hundred grains of pure calomel. I remember making a passing inquiry about a friend, with whom I had conversed the day before, while he was in apparent good health and spirits; the answer I received was, that he was dead and buried! Man, in India, may truly be said, in the emphatic words of Job, to flee as a shadow.

I had been absent from Bombay many months, and had returned again rather broken in health, after a sojourn into Western India, and an attack of its jungle fever; and as it was the height of the hot season, I determined, that till the rains should set in, I would take up my quarters upon the esplanade, in a tent which I had hired for the purpose. I was rather fortunate in getting this tent pitched within a few yards of high water mark—an advantageous position for a delicate person, and from the great demand for ground-room at the time, a very difficult one to secure, after the land had been staked out by the authorities. I was not without company, for a large number of tents had already been pitched, and a strange set of people lived inside of them; consequently to walk between the rows, and see what was going on among my neighbours, was a species of amusement of which I was rather fond. The tent on my right was occupied by two young officers, good specimens of the griffin-kind; quite boys in outward appearance, their white faces indicating their recent arrival on the island from some northern country. They seemed very anxious to get tanned as soon as possible; seeing that they were accustomed to spend the greater part of their day out in the sun; consuming during these idle hours so many manilla cheroots, that I fancied at times some wager must have been depending between them, as to how many they could convert into smoke in a given period. When not in uniform, or expecting a visit from a superior officer, they each mounted a large Arab fur cap, something in shape like a sugar-loaf, adorned by a red cotton top, that drooped down on the side and served as a tobacco-pouch. A white jacket, and what are used in India as sleeping trousers. or defences against mosquitoes, completed their attire; and there they sat opposite the fly of their tent for hours together, cracking jokes on every native that passed by, and collecting *Bohrah* men around them, under the ill-founded idea, that they were going to become large purchasers of their commodities. But in these sharp merchants they occasionally met their match, and once or twice the but-end of a large chittree reminded them that the Hindoo was not to be trifled with every day, however sweet his temper might be. The *Bohrahs* are the pedlars of the East, and gain a living by hawking about from house to house the different articles they pick up from the public sales, which articles are transmitted from place to place in large baskets, on the heads of Coolies. These itinerant hucksters spread out a mat by your tent-door, and display thereon an infinite variety of native and foreign merchandise. It would be impossible to enumerate a tithe of the strange things which they offer for sale. The five continents, one might suppose, had each contributed their produce to help in filling the *Bohrahs'* baskets. London goods, however, are honoured with much space here. Shirts are shown you at so much the dozen (often considerably cheaper than you can buy them at home;) socks, collars, swords, epaulettes, plated dish-covers, hot-water plates—much used in India, for the punkah starves your dinner—saddles and bridles, native toys, musical boxes, guitars, and even down to the penny yellow whistle, that delights the country child at an English fair; these, and almost all other things, are to be found in the Bohrahs' baskets. The owners of these baskets are often wealthy men. They abound in news; and as they speak English well, can give you all the current chit-chat of the island. They know every European resident; and perhaps more about private character, than to the individual concerned would be agreeable. If ever, therefore, you are at a loss for social information, the Bohrahs are the persons to whom to apply.

These Borahs are of Arab origin, and dress in the costume of their country. They call themselves Ismaeliah, from one of the many followers of Mohammed, who dwelt in the age immediately succeeding that of the prophet; and as they are amusing in their conversation, and have acquired the art of flattery, they are great favourites with some English ladies, and often succeed in running away with the greater part of their pin-money in gewgaws and native ornaments. They never will believe that you are poor, or unable to purchase their goods; and generally end their persuasions by saying, that "English saib very rich; always have little money to buy something of poor Borah." The Borah shows much anxiety to learn all he can respecting the manners and customs of the English at home. I remember one of them boring me for about three hours by asking me the most extraordinary questions relating to England; whether it were really true, that Englishmen travel in their own land without horses, bullocks, or *hummals*, (palanquin bearers,) as some saib had told him they did, and that the carriages they used were like the Company's steam-packets, and ran upon iron rails from one town to another at the rate of sixty miles an hour. I told him that it was even so; illustrating my description of a railway by a diagram; and after showing him that the motive power was the same in both cases, he, with the assistance of the drawing, at last thoroughly comprehended this, to him, hitherto inexplicable wonder. He never forgot to call and enquire about my health when he passed, and seemed to feel much the trouble which I had taken in revealing to him the mysteries of a locomotive engine. In fact, the Borahs all appear to thirst after knowledge, and are easily instructed.

The tent on my left was occupied by a captain in the army and his family. It was a very handsome double-poled one, and covered a large portion of the compound. Beautifully picturesque was it to look upon, but miserable and wretched were its occupants. The captain was a man of the most dissipated habits, and his poor wife and innocent children were treated like brute beasts by this monster in human form.

How he ever retained his commission, leading the dissipated life which he appeared to lead, was to me a miracle, for like all drunkards he was perfectly careless of public opinion. I think it was only my second evening on the esplanade, when I was disturbed by the most pitiful cries of a female in distress calling loudly for assistance; I ran out, and found that the voice proceeded from the captain's tent; and was about to enter it, when to my amazement, the whole of one side was forced out, and the poor lady followed by her children who were leaping off the tops of drawers and tables to escape from their father's fury, made towards my tent; the children, many of them half naked, taking shelter with the cadets above me. This tragedy was often enacted, and more than once I felt inclined to report him at head quarters as a nuisance to the neighbourhood, but I thought the poor family would in this case be the greatest sufferers. I have recalled it to memory simply as affording an instance of the results which often follow those unhappy marriages, which in India too commonly take place between English officers and half-caste women; and may here observe, that when such unfortunate unions occur in the army, both husband and wife are generally cut by the officers of the regiment to which they are attached.

With some trouble, and but little expense, for furniture is reasonably cheap in Bombay, I contrived to get my little tent snugly fitted up; Pedro, my Portuguese boy, appearing to take a great interest in arranging these matters to my satisfaction. He was a thin, slim lad of about eighteen years of age, with a winning expression of countenance, and short, curly, jet-black hair. His favourite dress was of Orleans cloth, and on Sundays and high days, he exhibited a very showy lace front to his shirt, which piece of finery, he said, had been the work of some of the old nuns in his native town of Goa. I often envied him two good gifts which he possessed in perfection. A splendid set of pearly white teeth, and the sweetest temper that boy was ever blessed with. He was conscientious, and truly honest; and, unless on occasion of a wedding, or a funeral of some relation—for he certainly appeared to have a good number of stray cousins—he seldom wished to go from home, except it were to mass, or the church service held in the neighbouring town.

Altogether, I was very well contented with this new way of living. The evenings were certainly long, and often tedious; but my health improved, and I contrived to pass them happily, by writing, and in company with those friends that never reproach one—instructive books; and during the day I was fully occupied. I had perhaps too much time for reflection; and the bitter idea of being separated from all that was near and dear to me, cast occasionally its dark shadow across my path, and made me feel as if I were alone in the world. One night, as I was poring (by the aid of a cocoa-nut-oil lamp, that was flickering in the air, in consequence of the number of drowsy beetles that kept humming around it,) over some old letters received from England—having nothing to disturb the solitude of my little home, save the snoring of Pedro on one side, and the heavy, uneasy breathing of my cook on the other—for they both slept between the passages of the tent, and had rolled themselves up an hour or two previously—my attention was rather suddenly arrested by observing the fly, or doorway, of my sitting-room gently moved on one side, by the hand, as I thought, of a man. I felt, for the moment, a little alarmed; but not again observing the circumstance, went on with the perusal of my letters; fancying that the movement might have been occasioned by a current of air passing under the canvas from the sea-shore. The Cathedral had tolled out the hour of eleven some ten minutes before; and I was preparing my couch for rest, when again I detected the movement of the fly, and called out, "*Carmunta?*" (Who is there?) when an ill-favoured-looking scoundrel put his head and shoulders inside the tent, and made me a salaam. As it was a time of night at which I had never before been visited by any of the natives, I was at a loss to account for the strange appearance of this man; and involuntarily grasping a small dirk-knife which lay on my writing-desk as a paper-cutter, I called loudly to both my servants; in a second they were with me; for native servants in India are very light sleepers, and are aroused in a moment. The man had by this time walked in; and after squatting down, seemed surprised to see me so agitated, as I must confess I was. Pedro, who was more alarmed than I expected he would have been, after bringing the lamp to bear upon his features, recognised him at once as the *ramoosie* who guarded my drunken neighbour's compound. The cook inquired his errand, and how he dared to intrude himself upon his master at that unseasonable hour. His answer was, that unless I hired one of his people to guard my tent, he would not answer for the safety of my property another night; that it was customary for all English *saibs* to do so; and that if I would promise to give him half the usual wages, three rupees a month, he would look after my tent as well as the captain's. As I had never before heard anything about these *ramoosies*, I asked Pedro if what the man told me were the truth; and as he confirmed his statements, I agreed for the sum named, and dismissed him. After passing a rather uneasy night, the following morning I sallied out early into the Fort, to consult a friend with respect to the hasty promise which I had made. He told me I had acted quite rightly; and that if I did not keep a *ramoosie*, I should assuredly be robbed; in short, that nobody lived in tents on the esplanade, or, in fact, anywhere in India, without them; and so ended the matter for the present. Four or five mornings after this unexpected visit, I was rather roughly awakened, just at daybreak, by Pedro, who had got up earlier than usual, and who had discovered, that the tent had been entered during the night, and that every portable article which it contained had been carried off, as if by the hand of an enchanter. He wrung his hands in the greatest sorrow, as he fully expected I should now give up living in tents, and dispense with his services. I hastened to rise, and found, upon inspection, that his tale was too true. Pots, pans, glasses, knives and forks, and books—all had departed. Articles within a foot of the camp-bed on which I was sleeping, had been cautiously removed, and carried off by the thieves. My first thoughts turned to my writing-desk ; for, besides the few rupees I possessed, it contained some remembrances that money could never restore. By a mere accident, it had escaped notice. The thieves had actually stepped over it ; the opening which they had made for themselves, by pulling up a tent pin or two, being immediately behind the valued desk.

Unfortunately, I was not the only sufferer, for the marauders had decamped with my cook's wardrobe ; and he certainly bestowed upon them some remarkable Portuguese denunciations, for robbing, as he said, a poor fellow like him. Pedro, as I found, had been more favoured ; for he had taken good care, every night, after the *ramoosie's* visit, to put all his valuables under his bedding, and, in particular, had made a pillow of his Orleans suit. My cups and saucers having accompanied the tea-kettle and teapot, I was necessitated to beg a breakfast from a neighbouring gentleman, who did not appear the least surprised on hearing of my losses. He said it was an every-night occurrence in Bombay, but advised me to give information to the head of the police force, which I did; but, from that day to this, I never heard anything more about the stolen property, though I was pretty well satisfied the thief lived next door to my tent. As it is commonly reported in Bombay that the native police are often implicated in these robberies, and that a regular systematic plan is followed up to prevent detection, I thought it but a loss of time and money to pursue this investigation further, though I did cause a district in the native town, known as the "thieves' bazaar," to be well searched. The amount of property annually stolen in Bombay being really enormous, it is astonishing that this gang of professed thieves is not put down by the strong arm of the law. Any attempt to capture any of these midnight visitors yourself, is quite out of the question. They enter your dwelling perfectly naked, with their bodies well smeared over with cocoa-nut oil; and any one daring enough to shoot or wound them, is said to become a marked man; and though years may intervene, you live in dread of ultimately falling a sacrifice to the smouldering revenge of these town Thugs.

Since the above was written, great interest has been excited in Bombay by an investigation of the conduct of the police. According to the Bombay Times, "the heads of almost every department in the establishment have become so deeply involved with natives within their jurisdiction as to be open to the gravest imputations. The chief magistrate exercised no supervision or control over the others, nor kept any separate records. Government property was sold to the chief creditor of the members of the establishment at half the price offered for it by others. The cash thus secured, was thrown into a box, into which were thrust all varieties of property which fell into the hands of the police—money, watches, jewels, specie, &c. and no one knew who kept the key; no account was kept of the goods, and a very small proportion of them seem ever to have been accounted for. The price of the property just referred to was received in 1846; up to the present time it has not been accounted for. Tenders made four years since by intending purchasers of police-property remain still unopened. Warrants were issued by the chief magistrate and remained for years unserved. One influential native *employe* was known to keep an extensive gambling establishment, where gambling was at all hours of the day seen by the police to be in progress—no one interfering. Crimes of all kinds were hushed up and compounded for; and the whole of the subordinates seem to have been in the last degree corrupt. "Such," observes the editor, "has been the system prevailing for years in the commercial capital of Bengal, under the very nose of government! Is it to be wondered at that belief in the corruption of the provisional police and police courts should be almost universal?"

And now I think I have exhausted my reminiscences of Bombay and its beautiful islands. I lay down my pen with regret, and if my readers derive but half the pleasure from the perusal of my little volume, which I have experienced in its composition, I shall feel amply repaid for any labour which it may have occasioned me.

In conclusion I would express my hope, that these "Recollections" may make some of my younger readers more satisfied with the land they live in. I would fain believe, that though England has its snows, and its long winters, its fogs and other discomforts, with which we are constantly finding fault, there are many, nevertheless, who would not willingly resign its solid advantages and real enjoyments, for all the glittering pleasures of the far famed East; half of which pleasures must, after all, be confessed to owe their attraction chiefly to the illusions of imagination.

THE END.